HITLER'S
U-Boat Bases

Jak P. Mallmann Showell

SUTTON PUBLISHING

First published in the United Kingdom in 2002 by
Sutton Publishing Limited

This revised edition first published in 2007 by
Sutton Publishing, an imprint of NPI Media Group Limited
Cirencester Road · Chalford · Stroud · Gloucestershire · GL6 8PE

British Library Cataloguing in Publication Data
A catalogue record for this book is available from the British Library.

ISBN 978-0-7509-4555-4

Title page photograph: Workers clean up on the quayside at Bordeaux as the bunker rises
across the river basin.

Typeset in Times.
Typesetting and origination by
Sutton Publishing.
Printed and bound in England.

HITLER'S
U-Boat Bases

Contents

Atlantic coastline.

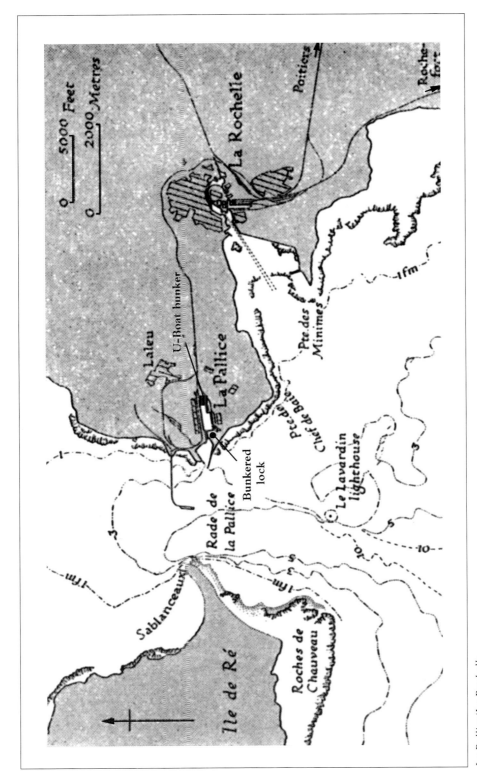

La Pallice/La Rochelle.

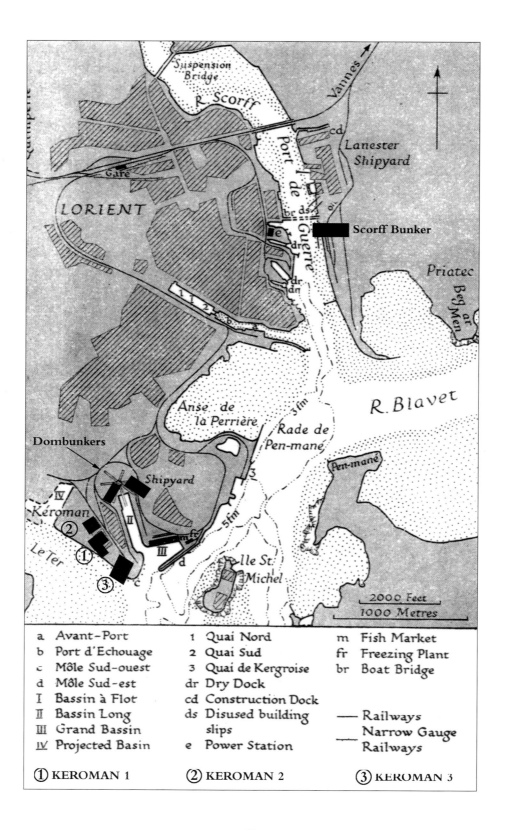

a	Avant-Port	1	Quai Nord	m	Fish Market
b	Port d'Echouage	2	Quai Sud	fr	Freezing Plant
c	Môle Sud-ouest	3	Quai de Kergroise	br	Boat Bridge
d	Môle Sud-est	dr	Dry Dock		
I	Bassin à Flot	cd	Construction Dock	——	Railways
II	Bassin Long	ds	Disused building	····	Narrow Gauge
III	Grand Bassin		slips		Railways
IV	Projected Basin	e	Power Station		

① KEROMAN 1   ② KEROMAN 2   ③ KEROMAN 3

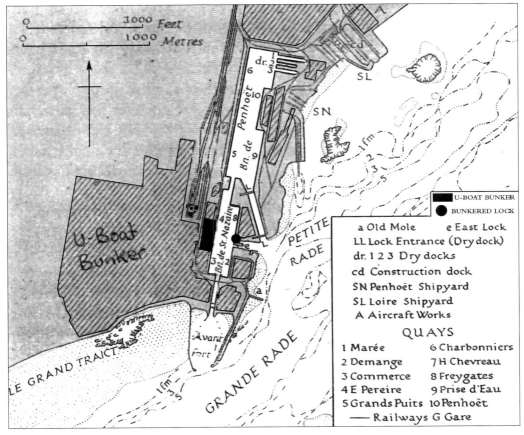

St Nazaire.

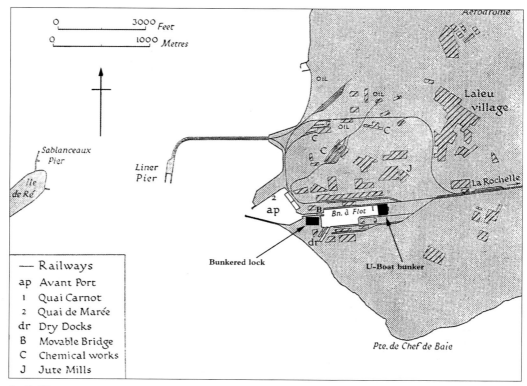

La Pallice.

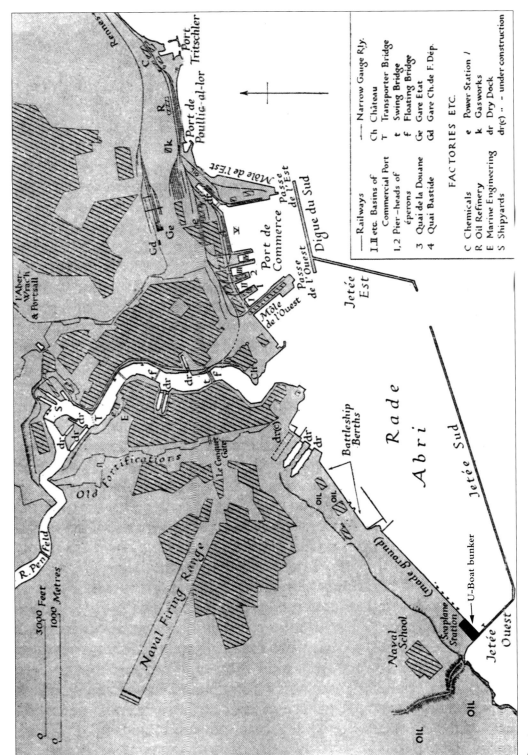

Brest.

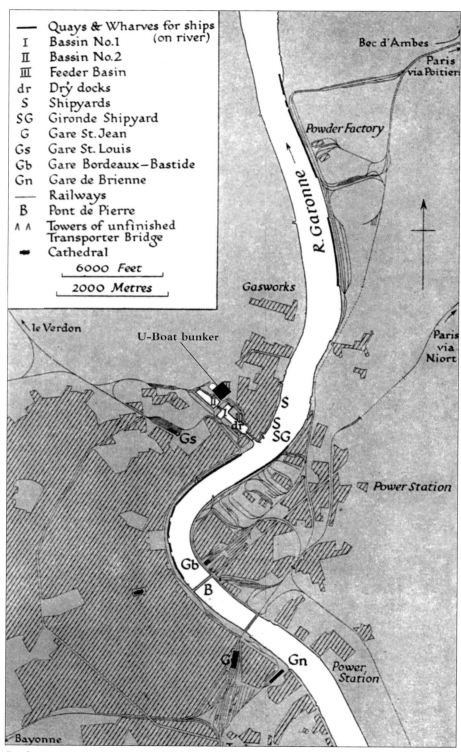

Legend:
- — Quays & Wharves for ships (on river)
- I   Bassin No.1
- II   Bassin No.2
- III   Feeder Basin
- dr   Dry docks
- S   Shipyards
- SG   Gironde Shipyard
- G   Gare St. Jean
- Gs   Gare St. Louis
- Gb   Gare Bordeaux—Bastide
- Gn   Gare de Brienne
- — Railways
- B   Pont de Pierre
- ʌ ʌ   Towers of unfinished Transporter Bridge
- ◄   Cathedral

6000 Feet
2000 Metres

Bec d'Ambes
Paris via Poitiers
Powder Factory
R. Garonne
Gasworks
le Verdon
U-Boat bunker
Paris via Niort
Gs
S
S
SG
dr
Power Station
Gb
B
G
Gn
Power Station
Bayonne

Bordeaux.

xii

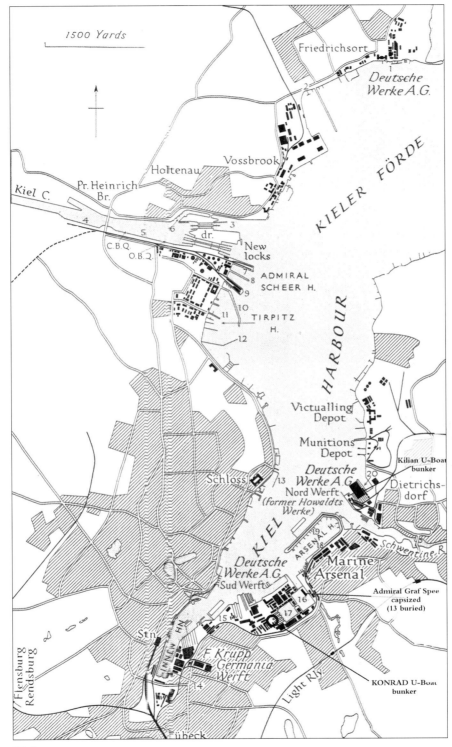

Kiel.

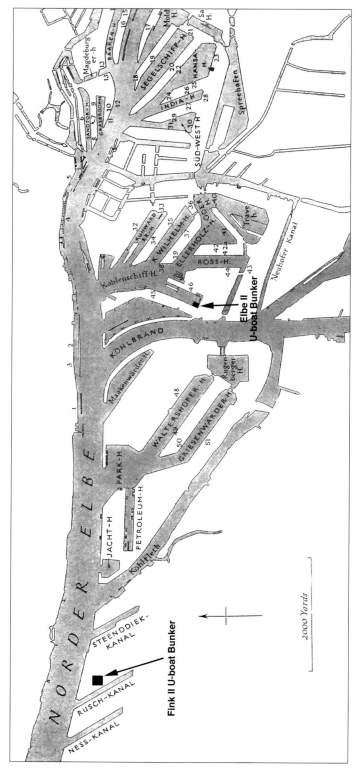

The docks at Hamburg.

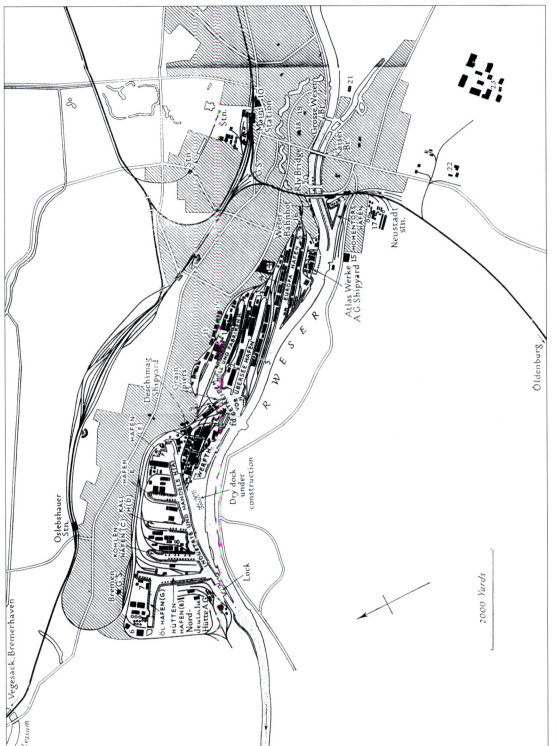

Bremen.

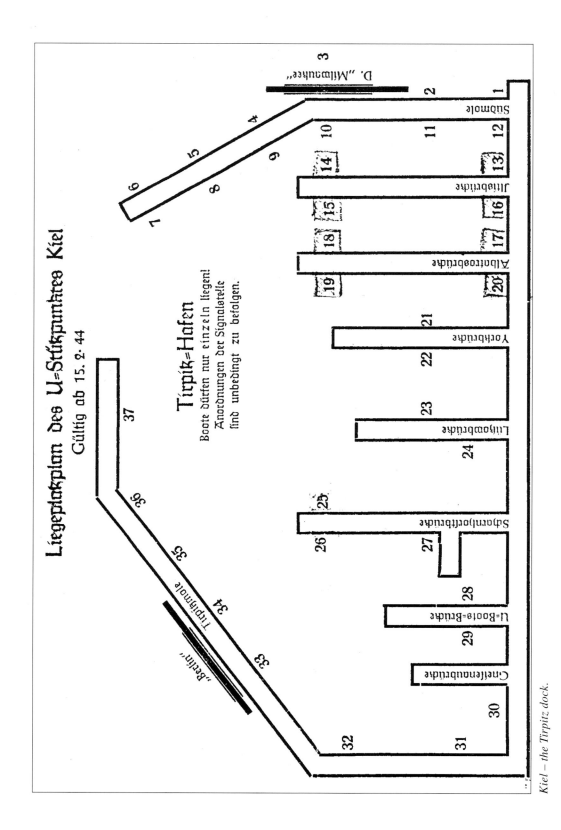

Kiel – the Tirpitz dock.

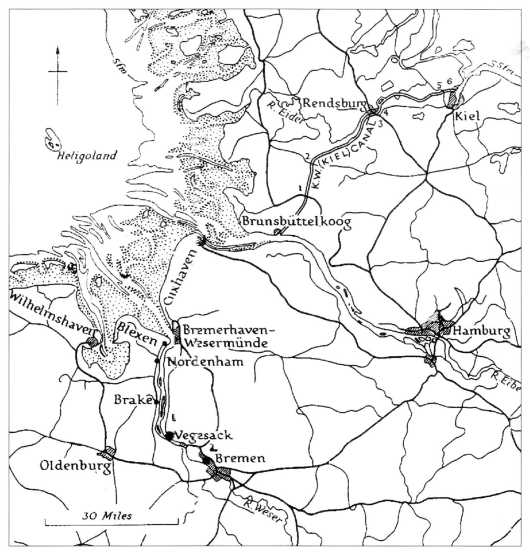

Heligoland, with (inland) Hamburg, Bremen and the Kiel canal.

Acknowledgements

This book is largely based on fieldwork following extensive research in the International Submarine Archive (Deutsches U-Boot-Museum) in Cuxhaven-Alternbruch and I am most grateful to Horst Bredow, founder and director of the Archive, for allowing me access to his collection and for guiding me through it. I also should like to thank Mrs. Annemarie Bredow and Horst Schwenk, whose knowledge and collection of rare publications has been most useful; Margaret Bidmead, for her help and for allowing me to scavenge through the library at HMS *Dolphin*, the Royal Navy's Submarine Museum in Gosport.

I am also grateful to my wife, Imke, for her terrific help in coping with the French language. (All the time and money spent on the Open University language course was well spent.) Jack Fletcher provided information from the Internet and Hermann and Elsa Patzke made sure we visited the numerous remains in and around Kiel. Knut Sivertsen, Professor Christen Christensen and Svein Aage Knudsen helped with information from Norway.

The maps in this book are Crown Copyright and come from British wartime accounts produced by Naval Intelligence and are reproduced by kind permission of Her Majesty's Stationery Office. The majority of the wartime photographs come from the Deutsches U-Boot-Museum in Cuxhaven, while the recent pictures were taken on colour film by myself and a few were supplied by people mentioned above.

Introduction

My curiosity on the subject of U-boat bunkers was aroused one cold December day in 1984, when Gus Britten and Commander Richard Compton-Hall at the Royal Navy's Submarine Museum in Gosport (England) asked me to help identify a U-boat from which a compass had been removed way back in 1948. This apparently innocuous investigation led me to make contact with Howaldtswerke-Deutsche Werft in Hamburg for permission to enter the ruins of the Elbe II bunker at low tide. The prominent historian and author of a unique diary, Wolfgang Hirschfeld, accompanied me on this fantastic tour, when we 'discovered' three U-boats lying side by side in the murky darkness under the collapsed roof. In many ways it was unbelievable. There they lay, on the surface, amid the biggest city in the Federal Republic. Herr Traband, who had worked with HDW for most of his life, had known of their existence for a long time; but the discovery by an 'outsider' was such a revelation at the time that the owners of the site asked us to keep the matter secret, to prevent a possible influx of sightseers and tourists into what was then a highly restricted part of their works.

Strangely enough, it was 25 years and 25 days later that Innes McCartney and myself accidentally bumped into Klaus Peters at the bunker. His job as official botanist for the Port of Hamburg Authorities took him around the port. Being interested in the redevelopment of the area, he was in the process of recording the changes on film. We were delighted that he also shared his vast knowledge with us.

I was also fortunate in meeting Ian Hansford at the Brooklands Museum near Weybridge in Surrey and I am most grateful to him for allowing me to have a copy of the magnificent thesis he has written about the history of the Tallboy and Blockbuster bombs. On this subject, I should also like to thank Ron Payne, engineer extraordinary, for showing me around the Brenzett Aeronautical Museum on Romney Marsh, where there are two suspected Tallboy tail fins. Their unusual appearance led me to the RAF Museum at Hendon in North London, where the staff kindly supplied some photocopies from official records. Martin Baggott, together with other members of the Buckinghamshire Aircraft Recovery Group, kindly explained what this information meant. The group has a fascinating display at Bletchley Park (or Station X), the home of British cryptography. They also helped me to make contact with Jim Shortlands, the official historian for RAF 617 Sqdr. The tail fins and a casing lying at Brooklands in Surrey turned out to be parts of nuclear bombs, rather than Tallboys, making their discovery even more fascinating.

Many U-boat bunkers still dominate their surroundings, so anyone wishing to explore these fascinating relics from Europe's turbulent past will have no great difficulties in finding them. Entering such stalwart fortresses while standing on the deck of a small U-boat must have been an awe-inspiring experience, yet very few photographs and only a small number of publications have ever appeared on these massive monstrosities. The Deutsches U-Boot-Museum holds well over 100,000 photographs, but there are very few unpublished wartime pictures of the bunkers. Somehow, the fascination which grew up around U-boats did not stretch as far as embracing these impressive fortresses.

The French, who now own the greatest number of U-boat bunkers, have also produced a number of interesting publications, but there are few books on the subject and the one and only comprehensive German work, that by Sönke Neitzel, has never been published in English. Luckily the Allies appeared to have been so impressed by the huge shelters that they commissioned a number of extensive reports as soon as they gained access to them and many of these unpublished accounts are now available for research. One also gets the impression that the Allies were so deeply frightened by these powerful bastions that they ordered the removal of the majority on German soil.

This, then, is the story of how they came to be built, the operations that were based there, and their ultimate fate.

Opposite: When looking at the awe-inspiring dimensions of U-boat bunkers, it is easy to forget that these were only a small part of a massive construction programme and a number of air raid shelters dwarfed even these huge monstrosities.

This shows the air raid shelter-cum-flak-tower next to Feld Strasse underground station in Hamburg. Until recently the outside was covered with black bitumen paint and the masses of windows are a post-war addition, having been cut during the late 1950s when the bunker was used as a broadcasting station and accommodation for homeless refugees.

The bunker is less than two kilometres or a couple of minutes flying time from the river Elbe, therefore the four 88mm anti-aircraft batteries on the roof would have been able to reach some of the bombers trying to hit the shipyards there.

I
U-boat Bunkers

THE BUILDERS

Open-sided U-boat shelters of the First World War, resting partly on wooden foundations, were built at a time when small bombs were dropped over the sides of aircraft by hand. Although British aiming had not improved a great deal by the middle of the next world war, the destructive power of bombs had increased so significantly that the Naval Construction Office in Berlin had already given considerable thought to the design of future bunkers. The requirements for these were established as early as the mid-1930s, at about the same time as Hitler was appointed Chancellor. For once, the diverse interests within the navy, which were so often prone to squabbling, agreed that such protection would be vital in any future conflict. Yet, when the war started these projects were pushed further down the line of priorities. This was partly due to a national atmosphere in which the building of air raid shelters for civilian use was considered to have been defeatist to the point of being subversive. It was not until one year later, when bombers from the Royal Air Force attacked a northern suburb of Berlin, that Hitler gave the go-ahead for the erection of three anti-aircraft towers in the Reich's capital. A few days later he instigated an enormous air raid shelter construction programme to make this one of the biggest building ventures of all time.

Bunker Valentin on the river Weser at Farge near Bremen is now used by the Federal German armed forces as a store, making access difficult. The area on the other side of the fence is patrolled by armed guards with dogs and there are ample notices saying that guns are used to protect the site. Despite this, it is quite easy to walk around the outside to get a good impression of this huge building. This shows the main gate and the landward side of the bunker, which is almost half a kilometre long.

Before the war it was common for groups of U-boats to make fast side by side in groups called 'Päckchen'. This was prohibited as soon as the war started because they provided too large a target for enemy aircraft.

For a long time Hitler held tightly to his firm belief that the war would be short and, wanting peace with Britain, went to considerable lengths to appease the government in London. It was only when these efforts failed, and the German forces were entrenched along the French coast, that the bunker building programme was given higher priority. Even then, it was still not considered necessary by the general consensus of opinion, especially those who put in their trust in the Luftwaffe. Reichsmarschall Hermann Göring moved the majority of his air force into France with the boastful claim that it would sweep British opposition from the skies. It was only when it became clear that the Luftwaffe could not gain air superiority and the invasion preparations were abandoned that the general naval policy of operating in French coastal waters changed. By that time, the only bunker under construction was Nordsee III, in a most vulnerable location on the island of Heligoland, some 60 km from the German coast. Preparations for a bunker in Hamburg, Elbe II, were also underway and these went ahead towards the autumn of 1940, a year after the beginning of the war. After that, others followed in rapid succession and the next three and a half years saw the consumption of almost 4.4 million cubic metres of concrete in France alone.

Such ambitious projects were beyond the capability of the navy, making it obvious from the outset that additional help would be required if these extensive plans were to materialise. Hitler suggested that the Todt Organisation under Dr Ing. Fritz Todt be entrusted with the administration of the labour force. This unfortunate name, closely resembling the German words for death and dead (*Tod* and *Tot*), helped Allied propaganda to portray the organisation as a group of depraved slave drivers. Yet such emotive garbage, as has often been written, is far from the truth. Sadly, it is not only

Karl Dönitz, the U-boat Chief, on the right and Fritz Todt, head of the Todt Organisation, on the left, being watched by an entourage of officials.

In Bordeaux, space was severely limited for accommodating the vast machinery needed to build the bunker and some of the cement mixers were such a long way away that the pipes had to be floated over the port basin on makeshift rafts, as can be seen in this picture.

wartime propaganda merchants but also postwar historians and even the erectors of stone memorials who have blotted their reputations by presenting wildly misleading information about the organisation. For example, a memorial in northern Germany states that two thousand people lost their lives while building the massive U-boat bunker at Farge near Bremen, giving the impression that they died as a result of ill-treatment by their German taskmasters. Yet, the inscription fails to mention that the majority of these were collateral victims of bombing by British and American air forces. Even that emotive word 'slave', which features so often in post war accounts of the Todt Organisation, requires some clarification because it conjures up a totally false image. For a long time we were told that the ancient galleons were rowed by masses of slaves until archaeologists rebuilt one in Greece and discovered that it took a considerable time before even highly motivated volunteers could master the task. A group of obstinate and underfed pressed men could never have succeeded in the strenuous and highly intricate teamwork required. The U-boat bunkers are among the most complicated structures ever built, erected exceedingly fast under the most difficult circumstances. The colossal undertaking required more skill and effort than an underfed, conscripted workforce could provide and the majority of labourers were volunteers who were offered considerable incentives in the form of additional pay and extra food rations to get the job done. So, what was the Todt Organisation and who were the builders?

Dr Fritz Todt was a civil engineer involved with the construction of roads until 1938 when Hitler asked him to organise the building of the West Wall. Called the Siegfried Line in Britain, it became a loose chain of anti-tank obstacles and gun emplacements along Germany's western border. Although quite substantial, it was nowhere near as massive as its opposite, the French Maginot Line. Many British people, living on an island, and Americans, as the events of 11 September 2001 showed, find it difficult to understand the mentality of nations who are surrounded by such hostility that they devote a large proportion of their income to the building of ramparts and other defences to protect their property and lives. Yet extensive fortifications have been a feature throughout Europe since the earliest of times and – though militarily futile – neither the Maginot Line nor the West Wall were by any means new concepts.

The Todt Organisation is quite difficult to understand, probably because there was no British or American equivalent. It was also unique in Germany, inasmuch as it had no ministerial or military standing. It didn't even have an official name, other than the identification which Hitler casually gave it shortly after coming to power. There was not even an official foundation day. One can look upon the organisation as a massive government Quango*. Yet this group grew from an administration employing just under 250,000 people in 1938 to running a vast workforce of almost 1.4 million by the end of 1944. Its objective was to create the necessary conditions for such extensive manpower to complete the tasks in hand. This involved recruitment, transporting the workforce to where it was required, accommodating people, feeding them, clothing them and

* quasi-autonomous non-governmental organisation, in its current usage.

Albert Speer, the Munitions Minister who succeeded Fritz Todt, on the left and Viktor Schütze, Chief of the 2nd U-Flotilla in Lorient, on the right.

Although arm bands were used throughout the Third Reich to identify officialdom, one wonders why it was necessary for members of the Todt Organisation to be labelled in such a manner.

providing incentives to prevent them from abandoning their work. Although the Organisation was involved with many small projects distributed widely throughout Europe, the main administration was carried out in a central office in Berlin. Fritz Todt must have been the type of engineering administrator every ailing firm dreams about, but he never saw the fruition of the many projects he initiated. He was killed when his aircraft crashed in February 1942 and was then succeeded by Albert Speer, shortly after he had been given the official title of Munitions Minister. The reason for the crash has never been ascertained and, although there is no evidence, Hitler's chief pilot, Hans Baur, who witnessed it, alluded to the kilogram of dynamite stored under the pilot's seat. This had a three-minute fuse for the purpose of destroying the aircraft if it had to make an emergency landing behind enemy lines. Although sabotage seemed highly unlikely, Baur pointed out that the detonation cord could have been pulled accidentally.

The construction of U-boat bunkers was not a bucket, spade and wheelbarrow job which could be undertaken by unwilling forced labour. It was a highly complicated, mechanised production process which relied upon skilled and co-ordinated teamwork from a large number of specialist firms. There were ample opportunities for sabotage to slow down the process or even bring the machinery grinding to a standstill, yet this rarely happened. Despite air raid warnings, workers often remained voluntarily at their posts to prevent the machines in their charge from clogging in their absence. Hitler was so impressed by positive reports about the performance of some foreign workers that he personally ordered that they should be well cared for. In fact, in the beginning the rations were so good that many of them put on weight as a result of the additional food they were given. Unfortunately, the disruption caused by the Allied bombing offensive curtailed the availability of supplies and things got slowly worse. It would seem highly likely that the majority of bombing raids on naval installations were indeed aimed at demoralising this massive itinerant workforce and designed to encourage them to desert. The towns and workers' accommodation suffered far more than the naval activities at the French and German bases, and resulted in a noteworthy migration away from French building sites. This international workforce, with no natural allegiance to Germany, was made up from many different cultures: North African Arabs, as well as men from virtually every European country, were represented. Many of these people had lost their jobs to the war and were keen to have an opportunity of earning a living from German construction projects. The paymasters went to considerable lengths to make matters attractive for them, such as arranging for part of the wages to be paid to the worker while another part was automatically sent to his family back home. This functioned so well across international boundaries that there were hardly any interruptions or delays in the receiving of these regular payments. This in itself was a major achievement when one considers the formality and red tape associated with any type of international transaction in wartime.

A number of Europeans from occupied countries preferred the idea of working on the French projects because it gave them a good standard of living and at the same time offered them the status of being in a priority occupation, from where they were unlikely to be sent as forced labour to more vulnerable areas. Many arrived as unskilled labourers without experience in the building trade and found themselves encouraged to learn new

Unlike bricks and mortar, a concrete structure had to be built out of wood first to hold the wet cement. The considerable weights involved meant that this shuttering could not be made from flimsy materials and carpenters had to produce high quality products, while working to painstakingly small dimensions of accuracy. This not only required a specialised workforce, but also an army of expert craftsmen to acquire and saw the timber to the right sizes. This shows the construction of Dora I in Trondheim.

skills which enabled them to be promoted to more responsible jobs where their wages doubled or even trebled to compensate for their enthusiastic contribution. It is also interesting to add that a noticeably large Spanish contingent made up of men who had fought against General Franco during the civil war were singled out for additional rewards because their devotion to duty went far beyond what the German construction experts had anticipated.

The term 'forced labour' needs some clarification because a number of historians have connected it to the emotional word 'slave' to suggest that Germany was the only country during the war which engaged in this type of practice. Yet, as far as possible, Germany looked for volunteers and even later, when the Todt Organisation was given permission to recruit from low grade prisoners in jails, the men were asked to come forward rather than being forced into the job. What is more, generous incentives were offered to those who did volunteer. Even British prisoners – 'other ranks' – were keen on working and there are a goodly number of escape stories involving officers who lamented the fact that the Geneva Convention prevented them from taking part in more interesting activities than just sitting around in prison camps. For a long time, it has been in vogue for the media to show in great detail what the Germans were supposed to have done to others, but they hardly ever mention what was done to the Germans. In view of this highly one-sided view of history it is to be expected that so many accounts make a point of emphasising that the German authorities employed 'slaves' as forced labour, but always fail to mention the positive sides of the story. For example, that the overstretched naval resources in foreign countries were also used to feed a vast number of destitute children. In any case, the conditions endured by the German conscripted workers were no worse that those experienced by the Bevan Boys, British youngsters who were conscripted to work in British coal mines. What is more, the large masses of German 'slaves' who were forced to work by the Allies after the war, had to endure even worse conditions.

When considering the conditions under which conscripted labour forces worked, it is necessary to compare these with the general living conditions in the rest of the country. Towards the end of the war, for example, many workers suffered from the results of Allied air raids because the administrative sections dealing with the highly complicated supply routes were disrupted or even destroyed. It is no wonder that this resulted in suffering on a wide scale. These comments have not been included here to suggest that the workers were treated with kid gloves. The hours were long and much of the work was arduous, despite having machines to do the really difficult, backbreaking jobs. The day shift started at 7am and did not stop until 7pm, except on Sundays when work ceased around midday, and the machines were kept running by a night shift as well. Pouring concrete was a 24-hrs-a-day job to prevent seams of weakness from developing inside the structures. However, it is unlikely that workers of other warring nations of the time enjoyed shorter hours or noticeably better conditions.

The walls of a U-boat bunker, probably in Bordeaux, before the roof was put in place.

Prisoners wearing their distinctive black and white striped uniforms, putting iron supports in place in the roof of the Valentin bunker. These beams had the advantage of requiring much less steel, but they had to be cast in special pressurised moulds. Hardly visible in finished structures, the cement was poured around them so that they became embedded in the thick roof.

Men of southern European or African origin working on the top of the bunker at La Pallice with the distinctive vents of the colossal power generating hall in the background.

Bearing in mind that many of the iron bars were two to three centimetres in diameter and a man was only strong enough to carry a short length of such heavy rod, cranes were essential. Some historians have suggested that the men guiding these in place were actually lifting them as well, something which was impossible because the individual units were far too heavy for a man to pick up.

The workers were first put up close to their place of work, with unoccupied schools coming high on the list of suitable buildings for conversion into dormitories. However, the Todt Organisation made a considerable effort to move men quickly into more comfortable surroundings. Some lived in specially constructed barracks while others were accommodated in private houses in surrounding villages. The type of accommodation depended very much on the people. Trustworthy Europeans found they had considerable freedom to move about as they pleased, while others were kept in guarded compounds. But this was not unique to foreign workers. Many German soldiers in foreign countries were also accommodated in guarded compounds from which they were not allowed to stray around towns on their own.

The itinerant workforce was only a small part of the overall project and it could hardly have done the job had not a large number of specialist civilian firms contributed towards the construction. Today, historians give the impression of the majority of French people having belonged to the Resistance which is hardly true. Germany owed a great deal to a vast number of French contributors to the war effort. There were few problems with the workforce in France, nor with the acquisition of machinery, nor the procurement of raw materials. It was only Norway which differed. There, people were far more reticent about helping the Germans and much more had to be done with imported labour. That is not to say that France supplied everything for the construction of the bunkers. Most of the steel for the reinforcement, for example, was imported from Germany, where it was in desperately short supply.

THE BUILDING

The initial planning started long before the designs were finalised and specialists in a variety of fields were sent into France and Norway to lay the groundwork for the projects. They had to find the right locations, carry out exploratory investigations to discover what the ground was like and determine the type of foundations likely to be required. Sources for cement, sand and gravel had to be found. Timber had to be acquired and new railway lines laid. This was not just a case of adding a few narrow gauge tracks, but identifying possible congestion in the existing network and building diversions around potential troublespots. There were, for example, a number of lines with an abundance of stations where regular stopping services could seriously have hampered the supply routes to the bunkers. Therefore additional tracks were installed to prevent the build-up of possible traffic jams. This was potentially quite a problem. The Keroman site in Lorient, for example, was visited by some 60,000 railway wagons during its short construction period. In addition to this, specialists' machinery such as floodlighting, piledrivers, cranes, diggers and cement pumps were required in unusually large numbers. It is essential not to compare the acquisition of this machinery with its modern counterparts. The last mentioned, for example, had been invented during the mid-1920s, making them still a considerable novelty when the U-boat bunkers were built. Shovels and muscle power still featured strongly in all types of industrial applications and the mechanical diggers of the time were cumbersome and temperamental, many of them powered by exceedingly noisy steam engines and steel cables, meaning they were not as common nor as portable as their modern counterparts.

The Germans were keen on forms and pay day was no exception. There was no way that money was just handed over, it had to be signed for and then the completed forms followed an intricate path of red tape to keep busy an army of administrators. Matters relating to pay were made complicated by issuing wages in several different currencies. But money remained the principal reason why most people worked.

Female entrepreneurs quickly found ways of making a living from the abundance of workers. Here a lady in Bordeaux has set up a stall selling hot chestnuts. Restrictions on this type of activity were quite lax and a number of such dealers were allowed on site. The main reason being that happy, content and well-cared-for workers produce not only better quality but they also get on considerably faster than those who are tied down by unnecessary regulations.

Spanish workers in Bordeaux enjoying a break. Somehow one would not associate southerners with clogs, but then the Dutch made such footwear famous because it was ideal for soggy ground and could be made quickly with the simplest of tools.

The Todt Organisation had no problems procuring contracts with French firms, many of which were only too pleased to find employment for their machinery and men, but this put the Germans into a difficult situation because it made it necessary to hand over highly secret plans and that could only be done with Hitler's personal approval. Despite ample opportunities for disruption and sabotage, the entire operation in France ran smoothly, often without interruption. The locals were pleased to welcome the foreign workforce as it provided an income for many and also kept the abundance of bars in business.

Once the acquisition of materials was underway, vast storage depots had to be created to stockpile everything until it was required. When this was sufficiently advanced, the groundwork on the building sites started. In many places, temporary cofferdams were built with massive pumps to keep the sites dry before excavators could be brought in to dig out the space for the foundations. Following this, the footings had to be put in and then the entire bunker built with wooden shuttering to hold the nearly liquid concrete until it set. Of course, masses of steel reinforcements had to be put in first, and this presented one of the major dilemmas. It would have been possible to build with less than half the quantity of steel that was actually consumed, but the German designers could not guarantee that the labour force would be skilled enough to carry out such intricate and painstaking work. So, despite a widespread shortage of steel, they opted for the more expensive option which could be put in place by unskilled men. As an interesting sidelight, these labourers have often been called 'steel benders' by post war historians. Indeed, photographs have been published showing these men with virtually no tools supposedly bending the bristling protrusions. The highly trained academics who made these statements must have led sheltered lives in ivory towers. Had they actually gone on to a building site, they would have realised that the massive steel bars were far too thick to be bent without substantial mechanical aids. Much of the steel was pre-fabricated away from the site on specially designed benches and only needed to be put in place by the workers.

The next process of pouring concrete continued ideally without interruption until the walls reached their final heights. At that stage, prefabricated metal beams were placed over the top to hold steel shuttering for supporting the next layers of concrete over the roof. Earlier experiments had shown that the roof should be smooth, without a camouflaging layer of earth. Such a cover would only add substantial protection if the concrete was buried deep enough in the ground. It was known that a thin layer of earth would help to increase the blast effect of bombs, the reason being that the soft strata helped to reflect the force of the explosion downwards, rather than allowing it to escape harmlessly up into the air. However, flat roofs created a particular problem of bombs bouncing off before they exploded, demolishing any features around the sides of the fortification. In many ways it was far safer for the bombs to explode on the top of the thick roof, where the blast would pass harmlessly over surrounding obstacles.

The thought of near-misses on the waterside creating large waves, which could wash into the pens and possibly down open hatches, was largely disregarded, although some bunkers had a protruding roof, in theory to prevent bombs from landing too close to the

Clockwise from top left: This steam train chugging through the Valentin bunker before the roof was put in place shows the immense dimensions of the cavernous interior, something which is very hard to visualise, even when looking at the mighty structure from the outside.

By the time the Valentin bunker at Farge near Bremen was being built, there was a distinct shortage of labour and the Todt Organisation was given permission to recruit from low grade prisoners in jails. Wearing distinctive black and white striped clothing, these people are easy to identify in old photographs.

There were times when finding one's way through the building site became quite a route march with hidden dangers for the unwary. There were vertical walls without safety rails for stumbling down, hissing and unpredictable machinery, slippery slopes and 'quicksand' in the form of liquid cement. A group of Spanish workers is returning to their workplace after a lunch break.

The bunker at Bordeaux at a time when the walls had been completed and the first trusses of the roof were put in place. These huge metal beams had a twofold function. They had to be strong enough to support corrugated iron sheets until the concrete set and the beams acted as reinforcements inside the solid roof. This method of putting up roofs had the disadvantage of consuming a vast quantity of steel, but could be put in place by unskilled staff using simple tools.

openings. It seems likely that only one boat was sunk as a result of water washing into a bunker. This happened shortly before the end of the war, when U4708 under Oblt.z.S.d.R. Dietrich Schultz, went down inside the Kilian Bunker in Kiel. In this incident, apparently, aircraft attacking the town on the opposite shore missed their target and dropped some bombs into the water. The resulting waves washed for about a kilometre across the harbour to flood into the pens. However, there is a contradicting report that the bunker's doors were blown off by an air mine and flung across the inside, seconds before the blast caused U4708 to sink. In an ironic aside to this incident, Oblt.z.S. Hans-Gerold Hauber was ridiculed both by his crew and by experienced workers for ordering U170 to be rigged for diving while in the bunker. Despite being contrary to standing instructions. this simple precaution saved U170 from sinking while lying next to U4708 during that fateful attack.

Bunker construction had hardly got underway when it was realised that roofs would have to withstand considerably larger bombs than the planners had anticipated and consequently plans went ahead to increase the thickness. Some bunkers also had a special set of beams, called bomb catchers, laid over the top to prevent anything hitting them from bouncing. At this stage of development, the designers also realised that the navy was in the process of building larger U-boats and new pens were made bigger to accommodate them. Long before the war, the army had determined the thickness of concrete by experiment, but their plans for defensive installations differed inasmuch

Many Norwegian fjords have tidal dead-ends where silt has collected for millions of years. This shows the foundations for Dora I in Trondheim being excavated at the end of such a tidal basin. Shuttering kept water out while this stage of the construction went ahead. However, the Germans paid for choosing an area with soft soil by having to sink especially large foundations.

A close-up of the eastern wall lying sideways on top of the concrete jetty with part of the roof just visible on top of it. Note that the roof did not fit flat on top of the wall, but the shallow indentations acted as mortise and tenon joints.

Below: Although the building of the bunkers involved some highly skilled crafts, with heavy machines doing much of the backbreaking work, manual labour was still the mainstay of the building industry and, at times, large gangs of navvies had to put in some hard labour.

that the exposure of a small target area to an attacker was one of the decisive points. Whilst this was sensible for gun emplacements and personnel shelters, there was no way that one could reduce the massive dimensions of U-boat shelters nor shorten the distances roofs had to span from one wall to another. Despite this apparent drawback, experts calculated that it might even be an advantage because the lack of supports would make the ceiling more pliable and the elastic effect could add to the strength. In view of this, the thickness needed to resist a 1000 kilogram bomb was laid down as 3.5 metres and it was argued that this could be increased to virtually any thickness by pouring more concrete on top once the first layer had set hard, assuming, of course, that the additional weight had been taken into account while building the supporting walls and foundations.

Bridging the considerable width of each pen was still a major undertaking. At first designers came up with steel beams which rested on top of the walls. Corrugated steel sheets were then placed across the base of these and concrete poured on top. Additional iron was incorporated as well to provide the necessary strength. The massive steel beams were, of course, necessary to support the incredibly heavy cement while it was still in its liquid state. In later years, another type of beam was introduced. This was a compressed, almost semi-circular concrete arch formed in a special mould off-site. The advantage of this was that only a relatively small steel core was required to produce the desired strength. However, the production was complicated and could not be undertaken by unskilled labour. Once full, the mould was placed under pressure and kept that way for several days until the concrete had set. Modern pre-cast concrete components are produced by this method, but in the 1940s it was still a relatively new and untried technique.

Having got the roof in place was not the end of the construction process. Steel doors had to be fitted, electricity cables laid, lighting installed, cranes assembled and a long list of other finishing-off work still had to be carried out. In addition to this, the sites had to be cleared of builders' clutter and railway tracks used for carrying building materials. In fact, it is true to say that none of the bunkers were ever totally finished. Maintenance and finishing-off started long before the buildings were completed and continued right up to the end of the war. The Allied air forces continued bombing the sites, leaving the areas around the bunker utterly devastated, but for most of the time hardly affected the insides. This meant that large teams of labourers were required to constantly maintain the necessary services.

The roof strengthening procedures for U-boat bunkers were not unique to naval construction, but reflected a widespread, national miscalculation in all types of bunker dimensions. Soon after bombing started in earnest, it was discovered that the ever-increasing size of bombs had made the first wave of air raid shelters virtually obsolete by the time they were completed. The first major shock in this direction came during July 1941 when a civilian air raid shelter in Bremen was punctured by a direct hit. The experts were not only surprised by their miscalculation, but also horrified by the result. To make matters even worse, rumours went around that the Royal Air Force appeared to be concentrating on hitting bunkers in already heavily bombed areas. This was almost

Building the bunkers was a 24-hour a day job, not so much to get the work completed on time, but to prevent seams of weakness from developing in the setting concrete by allowing one part to dry out before new, wet cement was added. This shows Bordeaux and emphasises the large scale of the lighting which had to be laid on, and switched off instantly when there was a danger of an air raid.

The metal supports inside the concrete were made from a large number of interlocking components and weaving them into place was quite a tricky job. During the 1960s British construction workers got over the problem of metal shuttering not fitting together very well by using welding torches to cut off many of the protruding iron hooks. Consequently, whole new housing blocks had to be demolished. This shows how easy it would have been for saboteurs to frustrate the bunker building effort, but there are hardly any records of any such action having been taken.

certainly not true, and 'attacks' on already badly hit areas were more likely owing to poor target identification and hopeless aiming from high altitude. While some of this risk was reduced by camouflaging high rise shelters, the same technique could not be applied to massive U-boat bunkers, where the only real alternative was to add layers of concrete to increase the thickness of the roofs.

THE BUILDINGS

There were four basic types of bunkers large enough to accommodate U-boats:

1. Covered locks for raising and lowering water levels
   Locks connecting floating or non-tidal harbours with the sea were potential death traps since there was no way U-boats inside them could avoid an air attack while water levels were being changed. Hence new locks with massive bunkers over the top were constructed by the side of existing facilities to provide the essential protection.
2. Construction bunkers
   Used for building new boats. The initial plans were to place the entire production process under concrete.
3. Fitting-out bunkers
   The building slips in Germany remained in the open air, but bunkers were built especially for finishing-off launched boats.
4. Repair bunkers and shelters for operational boats
   These accounted for the bulk of the construction. There were two types, built either on dry land where boats were hauled up on ramps or in water for boats to float in and out. The floating variety had both wet and dry accommodation with locking areas to pump out water in order to carry out dry-dock repairs. Many of these bunkers were high enough to enable aerials and periscopes to be pulled out and replaced. As a general rule of thumb one can assume that a fair proportion of narrow pens for accommodating only one boat at a time were of the dry dock variety, while 'wet' pens were often wide enough to hold two or even three boats side by side.
   British intelligence obtained from captured U-boat men gave rise to a few intriguing stories, none of which are true. A bunker at Le Havre, for example, was supposed to have consisted of a dry dock. U-boats floated in and then water was pumped out. This revealed a railway track with special bogey. Once settled on the carriage, another set of lock gates opened to pull the boat into a subterranean shelter which was also below the water line. Although quite ingenious, the practicalities of such a structure were beyond German capabilities and such bunkers did not exist. However, this wild notion is probably the basis on which rumours of a supposedly underground and underwater bunker on Fuerteventura (Canary Islands) were founded, but there is no evidence that it ever existed.

A camouflaged ship in one of the dry docks in Brest, a short distance to the east of the U-boat bunker. Initially there were ambitious plans for employing German surface ships in the Atlantic, but this idea was abandoned when it was realised that the French bases were too close to Britain for comfort. The first bombing raids missed the German ships and demolished nearby houses, but the bombing quickly became more accurate to pose a danger to the small fleet of large surface ships.

Putting in wall footings for Dora I.

And of course, there were also additional bunkers for use as command centres, observation posts, gun emplacements, ammunition stores, workshops, office blocks, personnel shelters, etcetera. Trying to identify the purpose of these from looking at their remains is difficult, but one can apply the general rule of thumb that any bunker with small doors was likely to have been for personnel and therefore served as air raid shelter, accommodation block or command centre, while anything with openings large enough for railway carriages or lorries was a storage depot of some kind.[1]

When construction started, there were no hard and fast rules based on experience, and designs were modified as the war progressed. In addition to this, a number of different innovations were tried out. Many of the individual pens were designed for specific purposes and therefore did not have a standard set of features. For example, although the majority were fitted with a gantry type of crane running on rails just below the ceiling, these varied considerably in their lifting power depending on the type of repairs to be carried out. The composition of the concrete varied according to the availability of natural resources and some of this showed fascinating innovation. For example, there was a definite shortage of gravel and other large aggregate in Hamburg. Rather than import this on a chain of river barges, the designers turned to a local power station and used ash from the furnaces, which was dumped as an unwanted waste product or used for surfacing roads in country districts, cycle tracks and sports fields. This ingenious concoction proved to be highly successful in producing light and somewhat flexible concrete, capable of withstanding heavy shocks without cracking. As a result, after the war a considerable industry grew up making concrete building blocks from fly ash.

In addition to the space for U-boats, bunkers included the following main features:

- A strong, bomb-resistant roof, thick walls and armoured doors
- Road and rail access with unloading facilities under cover of the roof
- Administration areas with medical facilities and lavatories
- Communications offices
- Offices for U-boat flotilla staff
- Accommodation for key workers and duty U-boat crews
- Generators to make the bunker independent of the civilian electrical grid and the rest of the naval dockyard's emergency supplies
- Ventilators to extract noxious fumes from metal working areas
- A defence system in case the bunker came under attack by special ground troops
- Anti-aircraft gun emplacements
- Stores for spare parts. (Explosives such as ammunition, torpedoes and mines were usually stored in separate bunkers, some distance from the main submarine pens, and brought in by lorry or railways when required)
- Oil tanks

[1] For a more comprehensive guide to German coastal defences in Europe, see Saunders, A. *Hitler's Atlantic Wall* (Sutton 2001).

- Water purification plants to make distilled water for batteries
- Electrical stores
- Spare part stores
- Electrical testing facilities
- Workshops for painters, carpenters, mechanical engineers, etc
- Heavy engineering workshops for items such as anchors and chains
- Radio testing and repair room
- Periscope maintenance
- Motor rewinding shop
- Compressor reconditioning
- Guard rooms.

THE SUPPORT STAFF

Dealing with specialist staff imported from home was relatively straightforward, but the foreign bases could not function without vast numbers of so-called 'unskilled' labour. What is more, many of the tasks these men had to face were not as unskilled as one might imagine. Instead, they had to learn complicated procedures exceedingly quickly, to become proficient at a number of skills people normally took years to develop. Sadly,

The wooden shuttering of the Dora bunker in Trondheim carrying pipes from the cement pumps. These worked relatively well, as long as there were no great air locks nor any solid lumps in the system.

Naval vehicle pools in both Germany and in occupied countries relied heavily on all manner of mechanical transport. Prisoners of war brought to France aboard a blockade breaker or supply ship are seen being transferred by bus from the docks to secure land-based accommodation

The west entrance at Brest with the so-called 'ladder to heaven' still in place. These crude structures carried the pipes of the cement pumps and were wide enough for men to climb up when the system jammed.

after the war, much of this massive support force seems to have vanished into obscurity, almost as if it had never existed. Yet, among the files of the Deutsches U-Boot-Museum is an interesting and well-illustrated document about one such person who helped to defend the bunker and dockyard at Lorient. Unfortunately, the author did not take the trouble to write his name on the testimony he left behind, so I have related it more or less in his own words. I have added some explanatory notes of my own, to make the story more easy to follow.

It was 5 February 1941, a couple of weeks before the first boats of the 7th U-Flotilla were arriving in St. Nazaire, that I turned up at the reporting station in the centre of Hamburg. When we assembled, it was around 15 degrees Celsius below freezing and still dark, but there was no need to hang around for any length of time. We were quickly marched off to the main railway station to loiter as an untidy rabble in the third class waiting room until lunch time, when our train was finally ready. Communications had already become a major problem, with traffic so frequently delayed or even lost that timetables no longer had any great significance.

On the one hand we were delighted to know that we were going to Beverloo in Belgium for our initial military training, but on the other hand we weren't so keen on the idea of having to go via barracks at Brake on the western shore of the river Weser for kitting out. Everybody guessed that a spell in a German military

Precision engineering workshops were accommodated inside bunkers.

establishment was going to be more demanding than the prospects offered by a romantic foreign base. It was still many degrees below freezing and there was no heating in the train, which seemed to take an eternity to make its way to Bremen and then on to our destination. The windows were partly iced up and we kept warm by singing. In a way, it was very similar to a school outing and the last time I had been on one of those was not all that long ago. Had my service with the National Work Front not been declared superfluous, I would still have been working somewhere else as a green school leaver, but now pressure on the Reich meant that I had to prepare for war.

It was dark by the time we arrived at our destination. So it was the next day before we were kitted out in blue naval uniform. It felt strange, however I must say that it gave me an air of feeling exceptionally proud, although I still had no clue about how to wear the gear and could not even tie the knot in the scarf. Suddenly everything was different to what it had been like at school and our lives became studded with naval tradition. The accommodation was not much to write home about. It consisted of a massive room with the floor covered in straw. Lying on it was prickly, but then it was too cold to undress and the chaff didn't penetrate through thick coats. It was necessary to get used to the shrill of boatswain pipes and the shouting of commands.

Having got us looking like sailors, we were herded off to the station again, but this time we were horrified to find that our transport to Belgium consisted of cattle trucks. There was a general shortage of all kinds of rolling stock and the general public would protest if they had to travel in such windowless wagons, but we were young and still too inexperienced to call ourselves soldiers, so no one was likely to listen to our protests. In a way, the authorities looked after us quite well by providing each car with a small stove and a vast pile of dusty coal. This eventually produced a small amount of heat, but hardly improved the complexion of our new uniforms. In any case, some of them didn't appear to be new and looked as if they had already been worn. It almost felt as if we were supposed to look for bullet holes in the vests left from the demise of the previous occupant. The trouble with our 'first class' compartment was that enough people had been squeezed in to make sleeping virtually impossible. In any case, it was a bumpy ride in darkness, with everybody being shaken from pillar to post as the train was jogged along at what appeared to be a snail's pace. Yet this was enough to keep knocking the chimney off the stove and to fill the wagon with a choking smoke which also made our eyes sting.

The training in Beverloo was looked upon as a necessary evil and in a way was different enough not to become boring, although it was most exhausting. Military precision type of drill had been abandoned while we concentrated on the basics for keeping soldiers alive and in harmony with their stressful and somewhat unusual surroundings. It is quite likely that we got off relatively easily because the Führer was preparing to invade England and we were part of his plan to cross the Channel. We were moved to Calais, to be accommodated in a large school in Rue des Ecoles,

The German Navy has a strong tradition of celebrating every possible event as it comes up and therefore had no great problems in devising entertainment for the workers, civilian office staff and military personnel in foreign bases. This shows the entertainment programme on the wall of a bunker.

Cooking was not only an essential but also a never ending job and many of the naval bases had to cope with exceptionally large numbers.

An underground ammunition depot with shells kept in sealed containers. They were designed for storage in precarious locations rather than deep down in the relative safety of a magazine. U-boat ammunition was usually stored in similar, but smaller containers.

but the training didn't stop. If anything, it intensified, while we performed everything at the double. We had hardly established ourselves in Calais when the order came to move out. God knows where to, but then soldiers don't ask questions and, although we didn't know where our train was going, we could at least work out where we had been by noting the names of the places as we passed through them. This time we had windows to enjoy the magnificent French scenery and it was much warmer so there was no need to huddle together to prevent frostbite. Although it had been quite a splendid journey, our arrival in a place called Lorient was greeted by the most appalling downpour. It appeared as if this was going to be our trade mark because our arrival in Beverloo also coincided with drenching rain. There were no opportunities for sheltering and it was a case of arriving in our temporary quarters somewhat damp and wet.

Of course, we all knew that Lorient was Germany's biggest naval base on the French Atlantic coast, but we had no idea what contribution we were supposed to make to the war effort there. We weren't kept in the dark for long. Soon it was made clear that the fire-fighting force had been there for such a considerable length of time that they deserved home leave. Therefore we were going to start our real time in the navy by standing in for them. This was supposed to have been a temporary appointment for four weeks, but then, at the time of our arrival, no one could foresee that fire-fighters were in even shorter supply than sailors and such

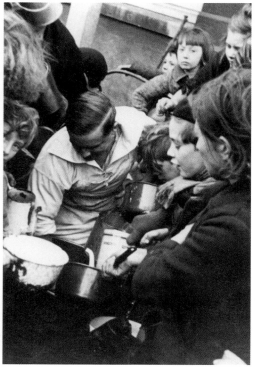

Clockwise from top left: A carpenter in action. Although woodworking is hardly associated with submarines, much of the interior cladding was made from wood and running repairs as well as modifications were often necessary. The craftsmen were usually under time pressure to get the jobs completed.

The powerful media makes a constant effort at telling the world what the Germans did to others during the war, but hardly ever mentions what was done to the Germans nor the plus points of the German armed forces. This shows naval volunteers feeding needy destitute children in France, many of whom have been made homeless orphans by Allied air raids.

The quartermaster's stores, one of the most essential parts of any naval operation anywhere. Not only did these places provide a vast variety of materials, but they also generated a fantastic amount of paperwork, keeping an army of administrators busy to assure that the stores did not run out of vital supplies.

Workers in Bordeaux agitating the last bits of concrete on the top of a high wall. This gives some indication of the iron's thickness and shows quite clearly that bending it by hand, without tools, would be impossible.

well-trained, strong men were urgently required elsewhere. God knows what happened to them, but they didn't come back and, although we were still technically part of the docks department in Calais, those couple of weeks of fire-fighting became a couple of years.

At first we were accommodated in Ecole Merville to become fire fighters for the naval dockyard. This would have been all very well had our group leader, a certain Bootsmann 'X', not been such a bloody sadist who could not tolerate us coming back from training or engagement unscathed. He wasn't content until out clothing had been torn and marked by a good saturation of filth and blood. No serious wounds, but enough scratches and bruises to make life uncomfortable and to develop a strong dislike for the evil fellow.

It didn't take long to experience a few ferocious air attacks, although the bombs seem to have done us very little damage. It appeared almost as if the English weren't interested in our cock installation, but wanted to get their revenge on the French for putting up with our presence. A good number of their houses were demolished. Even some of the blasts from a long way away were quite powerful. One of them threw me against a wall, causing noticeable bruising of the ribcage. Watching these raids from the rooftops of our harbour buildings was not the ideal way of surviving the war and I was pleased when the opportunity arose to join a bomb recovery squad. It was absolutely staggering to see the vast number of bombs which came down without going off. On one occasion, a dozen or more aircraft

The construction and maintenance of bunkers is often associated with masses of unskilled workers, yet these could never have done their jobs had it not been for an army of administrators. This shows the bunker control centre at St Nazaire with Oblt.z.S.(Ing.) Walter Stahl (Second Engineer) on the left and Oblt.z.S.(Ing) Maertens, (Third Engineer) on the right. Behind them are the charts with the complicated schedules to keep jobs running in the most effective order.

dropped a hell of a lot, but not a single bomb detonated. Dealing with these duds was not an easy matter, since a good number buried themselves quite deep in the ground and it was not advisable to get at them with a mechanical digger. Instead, it was a gentle pick and shovel job with greatest emphasis on the last mentioned. In the first eight days we succeeded in laying our hands on 27 unexploded bombs for the bomb disposal squad to deal with.

Of course, this formed only a minor part of our job and there were plenty of other tasks to be completed. In addition to this work of helping with the war effort, we still went through a most intensive training programme where we were acquainted with weapons, respirators, vehicles and a vast number of other mechanical gubbinses. Our weapons were a major part of the performance and it almost looked as if we had to be ready in case the English walked in and took over our places of work.

Things had been going pretty well, with hardly a great deal of thoughts of home when, quite unexpectedly, my group leader told me that I had been given a few days' home leave. Taking full advantage of delicacies on sale in France, I used my pay to buy some nice things such as bottles of cognac, some decent wine and a few

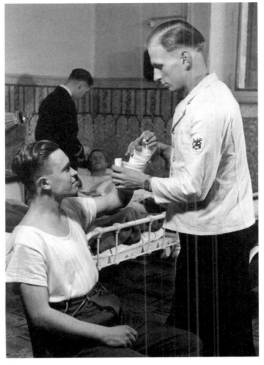

Clockwise from top left: Besides dealing with many injuries caused by enemy action and mountainous seas, the German medical services were stretched to breaking point with a large number of normal illnesses.

'House Atlantic' at Kiel-Wik, used as headquarters for the 5th U-boat Flotilla in Kiel until air raids made such buildings too vulnerable and vital offices were moved into newly constructed bunkers.

Although primarily U-boat bases, many of the occupied ports were supported by a multitude of back-up services without which U-boats could never have existed in foreign countries. In and around Brest there were at least fifty-two 105mm or larger and sixteen 88mm anti-aircraft guns, as well as a multitude of smaller calibre weapons to cope with low level attacks. This shows large shells being prepared for action.

alluring cheeses. The journey via Trier to Hamburg was uneventful until I returned home to find I had arrived just after a major air raid. The area where we lived was pretty well demolished and my family was pleased that I turned up just at the right moment to help clear up!

Having got back to Lorient, I discovered that we were due to remain in town and I was given the opportunity of manning a new set of offices. In October of 1941 our group was allowed to leave the barracks in town and take up residence in a fine villa at Rue Faidherbe, Number 2. From there we waged a paper war of considerable proportion, shifting vast quantities of official forms. This was quite comfortable until the end of the year when our work was suddenly suspended and we found ourselves being employed by the Todt Organisation to man cement mixers, to drive steam engines and to do some diving in the harbour. The massive building site resembled chaos on a grand scale, but one could see progress being made. Yet, despite having left my mark on the construction of the U-boat bunker, it was great to be shoved into a more appealing position with the air raids protection officer.

Having taken up this position, I was promoted to Matrosengefreiter (Able Seaman). I felt proud. It was the first step up the ladder to becoming an admiral. It was a grand feeling. One advantage of this new work was that we had to look presentable and we were often called upon to take part in the receptions for

Lager Lemp or Camp Lemp near Lorient with hut-like accommodation for visiting U-boat crews.

incoming U-boats. I became involved with the keeping of records, maintaining a photographic library for a war correspondent and attending the usual funerals and promotion parades. Following my promotion I joined a group in Lanester as air raid warden. This was pretty straightforward, but now I had been promoted I found it harder to deal with those colleagues who had joined up with me, but who had not yet been given a stripe on their arm.

The rest of the year passed without too much trouble. It was hard work, but hardly life threatening. It was not until the beginning of 1943 when we learned from a French radio station that the English air force had made it their main aim to raze Lorient to the ground. We laughed at the idea, although it did give us pause for thought. It was shortly before midnight of 14 January when we were suddenly aroused by the bone grinding sound of air raid sirens. Jumping up, as we had done many times before, we hurried down to our allocated space in the shelter. There was time to glance up into the sky to see masses of what looked like illuminated Christmas trees hanging in mid-air. Less than ten minutes later we experience a frightening bombardment of a type none of us had ever heard before. Incendiaries as well as high explosives were dropped, turning Lorient into a brilliant, huge fireball. There wasn't much we could do about it, other than wait for the best part of two hours before the commotion subsided and we were allowed out again.

The strange thing about this whole experience was that our places of work had hardly suffered at all. Everything remained in the best of order and we could continue virtually as before. But we were not left in peace for long. The next air raid was announced by those penetrating sirens at 8 o'clock the following evening. It was already dark as the English started with their destruction, and this time we could not get into the shelter. The sirens were still howling when we received orders to report immediately with our firefighting gear to the naval hospital to tackle a large blaze. Despite bomb splinters and anti-aircraft shells raining down, everybody concentrated on focussing water jets on the source of the trouble. This was not so easy because the main fire was surrounded by a mass of incendiaries, which did not seem to go out when they were sprayed with water. Instead they crackled and flared up more brightly. They were not too much of nuisance, it was relatively easy to pass between them, although there were several times when we abandoned our firefighting and scattered to take shelter behind anything solid.

The biggest danger came from an unexploded bomb which hit the roof near where we were spraying the timbers. The force of the impact very nearly flung us down to the ground, but thank God the device didn't oblige by exploding as well, otherwise I would not be writing this account. Having dealt with the hospital, we thought that we could limp exhaustedly back to our accommodation for some rest, only to find that there were orders to make our way down to the docks. A warehouse full of timber had caught light and required every available hand to stop the blaze from spreading. Somehow, we didn't get a great deal of time for rest after that and life became one drawback after another.

MOVING IN

Life for the dockyard staff was hard enough, but at least they did not have to put to sea. The U-boat crews, officers and other ranks were obliged to work from the new bunker complexes, often in foreign countries, and rapidly established their own operational routines. The following account, based on research by Korvtkpt Herbert Sohler, with additions by Kptlt Hermann Schlicht, graphically describes some of the problems and successes encountered while taking over command at St Nazaire. Commander of U10 and U46, Sohler later became Chief of the 7th U-Flotilla there.

Way back in 1936, when the flotilla network was originally established, it was thought that U-boats would operate in groups, like other small units such as torpedo boats and destroyers, where a tactical commander controlled activities from one of the boats at sea. In view of this it was important to establish the necessary administration structure so that the all-important backup on land continued to run smoothly while the flotilla was in action, often a considerable distance from base. However, when the war started, it was quickly discovered that U-boat battles could easily be controlled by radio from a land-based room and consequently the U-boat Operations Department mushroomed into the main command centre for the vast majority of activities in the Atlantic and far-flung oceans. At the same time,

These prefabricated, hut-like buildings in Lorient, used to accommodate the 2nd U-Flotilla and visiting crews, were quite comfortable inside and provided luxurious facilities compared to the Spartan existence aboard U-boats.

The east entrance of Tirpitz bunker in Kiel, which became the headquarters for the 5th U-boat Flotilla. The German Navy had a goodly number of brilliant heroes, but the higher authorities kept falling back on the same few traditional names such as 'Tirpitz'.

The west entrance at Brest with a number of dignitaries, war correspondents and steel helmeted guards. The huge armoured steel door blends exceedingly well with the murky colour of the concrete, but is visible towards the right of the picture.

Hotel Celtic at La Baule near St Nazaire which served as accommodation and mess for staff officers of the 7th U-Flotilla as well as visiting U-boat commanders.

individual flotilla chiefs lost their prospects of operational control and began focussing on the necessary support needed to get the boats into action. To this end they established themselves in the main bases, often aboard depot ships, where they dealt with everything boats were likely to need while replenishing in port. This, of course, was so vital that it could not be interrupted by moves to bases in foreign countries. Such moves were made easier in 1940 by the fact that the relatively little opposition for U-boats meant many did not require serious dock yard repairs when returning to refuel, but it was obvious that the full support of other services would soon be required if Germany was going to squeeze any advantages out of the newly acquired garrisons.

To accomplish the move, the 7th U-Flotilla in Kiel requested a train from the German State Railways for loading with the vital materials to establish the new base in St Nazaire, some 1500 kilometres away. Lorient was already in operation at this time, therefore the men had the advantage of being able to fall back on the advice and experience of others. Moving base meant carrying tools, spare parts, provisions, people and guards to create a fully self-contained, mobile unit. It was not known for how long the train would be on the move, but a journey of several days had to be taken into account. Therefore the wagons had be fitted with a restaurant and everything else which was likely to be needed to survive through potentially hostile terrain. What was more, this was not just a one-off for the 7th

A school in France used as emergency accommodation for advance parties and bunker construction workers. Later the building also provided accommodation for U-boat crews. However, the dangers of persistent bombing raids made the Germans evacuate this somewhat vulnerable location for safer places further away from the harbour.

The main entrance of the Casino at La Baule, was used as a mess for warrant officers as well as central kitchen and the large hall was converted into a theatre with access for military and civilian staff in the area.

This somewhat peaceful scene of the seafront at La Baule near St Nazaire, with an unexpectedly large number of cars, was photographed at the height of the Battle of the Atlantic on 27 June 1943.

U-Flotilla. A supply train was going to be needed on a regular basis, not only to carry supplies to France, but also to bring U-boat crews home for leave. Known later as the 'B.d.U. Special' (Befehlshaber der Unterseeboote or Commander-in-Chief for U-boats), the service ran a regular schedule between the Atlantic bases and Kiel. The trains were driven and controlled by staff from the German State Railways until they reached the border, where French staff took over, but the Germans remained on board in a supervisory capacity. The trains were often so full that it was not long before lorries with trailers were called in as additional support to help carry goods. Rumbling for days on end over rough cobblestoned roads, where they hardly ever reached a speed of 60 kilometres per hour (40 mph), they carried less sensitive items such as the personal belongings of dead U-boat men and mail for delivery to a post office in Germany. It must be remembered that, until many years after the war, France and Germany were renowned for the poor state of their roads. The journey can now be accomplished along motorways during one long day, but during the war it often involved at least three overnight stops on roads narrower, and often in worse condition, than the majority of modern country lanes.

The first train to pull into St Nazaire station, during a late morning in February 1941, received a rapturous reception from the advance party, which had already been there for some time, establishing the essentials to accommodate goods and personnel. Self-loading cargo with personal baggage was quickly moved by a fleet of vehicles to the seaside resort of La Baule, some 10 kilometres to the west. The rest was put under guard and eventually unloaded into a warehouse by the side of the non-tidal port basin. Transferring these goods was no easy matter, especially as they contained a number of highly secret packages as well as some bulky items such as a good-sized launch, capable of running out into the, at times, choppy estuary.

Finding accommodation was not terribly difficult, although the Luftwaffe had precedence and had already requisitioned some of the bigger hotels. Since there were no noteworthy air forces in the area, these buildings remained unused to be handed over to the navy some six months later. Hotel Majestik on the sea front served first as flotilla headquarters as well as accommodation for officers and it also provided rooms for in-coming U-boat commanders, while smaller hotels were requisitioned to accommodate other ranks. The holiday trade had been somewhat idle since the beginning of the war, when free and easy movement became difficult, and one gets the impression that the hotels were pleased to put up the masses of German guests arriving on their doorsteps. On the whole, the hotels continued to function with their own civilian staff, which provided some quandaries for security officers and made communications a little confusing, but Hotel Majestik had a German-speaking manageress from Alsace who ironed out most of the language uncertainties. In addition to this, there were a good number of interpreters, one of them a Russian with the name Herr Saizu.

The flotilla had to set up a vast variety of services: a registration room for open materials and another to handle classified matters, a printed paper store, an administration office, a personnel department, an engineering bureau, a post room and a number of other supporting services, such as a clothing depot. It was not just a case of stockpiling new uniforms, but repairing worn items and providing cobbling facilities. Again, much of this work was carried out by civilian French staff, but they all needed their own workshops and have them fitted out with the appropriate tools. In addition to this, it was often necessary to provide these workers with accommodation and food.

A medical centre was set up under the leadership of Marineoberstabsarzt (equivalent to Korvkpt.) Dr Rundte. This not only treated the sick and wounded, but also made serious examinations of every U-boat man coming in from an operational tour and carried out a similar inspection before he put out to sea again. The existing local hospitals would hardly have coped with such an additional influx, therefore one of the hotels in La Baule was converted into a naval sanatorium. Britain benefited from this establishment by having its wounded from the St Nazaire raid treated there.

All this was hardly possible without easy access to transport, especially as the quarters in La Baule were at least 10 kilometres away from the docks in St Nazaire. To this end, Oblt.z.S. of the Reserve Botsch built up a splendid vehicle pool, consisting mainly of French coaches, lorries, cars and motor cycles. This was backed up by a German controlled maintenance section. Interestingly enough, a large proportion of the drivers was made up of elderly Russian volunteers.

A small calibre anti-aircraft gun sheltered by makeshift sandbags, guarding part of the Channel coast of France. This type of scene was repeated over and over again along the length of German-controlled coasts and consumed a fantastic amount of badly needed resources.

Men from U198 celebrating in front of the bunker at La Pallice with the portcullis type of door clearly visible in the background.

Admiral Otto Ciliax, the German Fleet Commander, and Admiral Angelo Perona, the first Italian Submarine Chief in Bordeaux, 15 July 1941.

Men from U228 posing in front of the bunker at La Pallice. The original structure, consisting of seven pens, can be seen towards the left. Pen number 1 is hidden behind the crane and is not visible. The jetty in the distance was once the far side of the dock basin until three pens were added on that side. Once these were complete, that part of the basin was dug out to widen the floating harbour.

The domestic side of these arrangements developed quite rapidly and additional facilities were soon set up. These included a canteen, similar to British NAAFI stores, where all ranks including civilian staff could buy essential items at reduced prices. It might just be interesting to add a few prices from their drinks list. Immediately before the war, the average wage of a German male worker was 158 Reichsmarks per month, while women generally earned about RM 92. Light coloured, heavy alcoholic drinks cost RM 0.10 while dark coloured drinks such as whiskey and cognac cost RM 0.12. A bottle of white and red champagne was RM 0.90 and RM 1.10 respectively, while a large bottle of beer came to RM 0.45. Once the domestic staff had settled in, it became the general practice for everybody in naval quarters to take breakfast and an evening meal in the same hotel where they lived, while lunch was served in a canteen closer to their place of work. In La Baule, the Casino was converted into a massive dining hall with common rooms for this purpose.

Reading reports such as the ones written by Herbert Sohler and Hermann Schlicht, one cannot help but be impressed by the efforts made to make life comfortable for both Germans and foreign workers. These accounts make it clear that everybody was faced with a difficult task as well as additional stress, and the best way to achieve good results was to ensure that every person within that vast organisation was well cared for, happy and content. Otherwise the whole venture of operating out of foreign bases was bound to

Recreation kept the men from rougher pursuits, and sporting fixtures were always popular.

slide down the slippery road of failure. Schlicht, for example, goes to some lengths to describe how recreational areas were chosen with good views of the sea and how these were separated from other parts of the hotel by a considerable quantity of living plants, all of which required a considerable effort to maintain.

The operational side of the activities in the naval base was almost as complicated as the domestic arrangements. It was common for U-boats to be met at a predetermined rendezvous far out at sea to be escorted by a Sperrbrecher and boats from the Coastal or Port Protection Flotilla. The Sperrbrecher was a merchant ship filled with flotation aids and special facilities for the crew to withstand blasts from detonating mines. The idea was that these should sail in front of the more vulnerable submarines. At first U-boats entered through the small, western lock where an army band and a reception party were usually waiting. From there the boat was allocated a berth and coaches stood by to take men to their quarters. This small procedure alone required a considerable army of organisers to make everything run efficiently.

Initially, many of the staff working in the town of St. Nazaire were accommodated in an old city centre school which had already been used by the advance party to establish the facilities. Although much of the dockyard continued to function with its original French workers, German staff were brought in to cope with the highly technical nature of U-boat repairs and this could have been quite a problem, especially if one considers that many of the Germans didn't speak French and most of the workers didn't understand German. On top of this, spare parts were brought in from as far away as Kiel, placing the French bases not only at the end of a long supply chain, but also putting them in the highly precarious situation of never knowing when deliveries were likely to arrive. It was not long before much of the transport system was disrupted by incessant air raids on the railway lines as well as on the German production centres. Yet, despite these problems, everything functioned extremely well, which is a great achievement.

All this required not only a highly efficient administration system but also a quick means of communication. Since it was naval policy to shut down ship-based radio rooms as soon as the vessel entered port, it was necessary to lay new telephone and telex lines. This may sound somewhat insignificant, especially now where portable phones have made such vast inroads into life, but in those days the majority of private houses would not have had a telephone and a number of businesses functioned without them as well. Many of the flotilla staff had to be reached day and night, making quick and reliable communications through landlines a vital part of the war effort.

Life was not always as smooth and sweet as this account might make out and a personnel reserve became a vital part of the flotilla's set-up. This was necessary because U-boat men fell ill, were injured or became unfit for service. Therefore they needed quick and instant replacements. In addition to this, there was a need to maintain discipline and the flotilla staff had to cope with a number of offences such as falling asleep while keeping

Cranes towering over the massive Bergen bunker complex in Norway, where work is nearing completion.

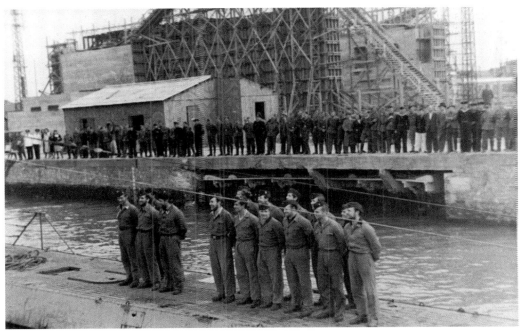

Men parading on the deck of U571 as it passed through the lock at La Pallice. The scaffolding in the background shows the bunkered lock under construction.

Sand and gravel being delivered to cement mixers inside the large Valentin bunker at Farge near Bremen. Mixers were accommodated in sheds by the side of the bunker so that the wet concrete could be pumped to where it was required, but this was not always possible and highly precarious road and rail systems were constructed to bring in vital supplies.

Apart for the massive Normandie Lock, there were two ways of getting into the floating harbour at St Nazaire. This shows U590 entering through the larger, southern lock at the end of the long harbour. The old pumping station, just visible towards the top left, is still standing. The slightly arched structure above and slightly to the left of the conning tower is the road bridge which has been swung out of the way. Behind it, towards the right, are two sets of lock gates. The inner set were too small for the majority of traffic and therefore another set was added further out to lengthen the basin by a few metres.

lookout or smoking or sitting while on duty to the more serious offence of having unprotected sex. The possibility of passing on a number of highly contagious, and at that time rampant, diseases was indeed a great problem. Discipline in port did occasionally become a headache, especially when drunken U-boat crews, who had just been to hell and back, realised it might well be their last time in port and they might never again enjoy close contact with someone of the opposite sex. Margaret Wiese, a secretary from the naval dockyard in Wilhelmshaven who was transferred to Brest, wrote home to her mother saying that there was no danger at all of running foul of nasty Frenchmen, but it was important to avoid wild U-boat crews. Meeting them could be highly unpleasant as some of them were so drunk that they could not walk unsupported and were likely to urinate anywhere. On top of that they tended to have the idea that any female, no matter what age, was only there to satisfy their personal sexual urges.

Many of the potential discipline problems were nipped in the bud by providing adequate supervision and a good entertainment schedule. Each hotel, for example, had a German officer in charge. He was often a U-boat man from the First World War and thus provided the type of father figure young men could look up to. Entertainment was not so much of a problem in summer when the majority of men drifted over to the beach to enjoy the sunshine, but in winter La Baule was somewhat different and cold dark nights with damp or even exceedingly wet winds sweeping in from the sea forced the staff of the 7th Flotilla to find ways of occupying men's time to prevent idle and boisterous hands from getting into trouble. Having made this point, it is important to state that discipline was hardly ever a major issue, but one of those things that could easily have got out of hand, had the senior authority relaxed its grip on the younger men. After all, many of them had only just come out of school and were away from home for the first time. They were bound to behave like a bunch of wild students, out for a good time.

It would appear that the first boat into St Nazaire after commissioning was U46 on a quick social call from Lorient during September 1940. U46 had been the flotilla chief's second command and the boat with which he gained his Knight's Cross. In May 1940, he handed it over to Kptlt Engelbert Endrass, the first watch officer from U47 (Kptlt. Günther Prien). U46 was also one of the first boats to call on the 7th U-Flotilla in St Nazaire on business, when it was refuelled with U48 (Kptlt Herbert Schultze) and U96 (Kptlt Heinrich Lehmann-Willenbrock). U96, the first of the trio to arrive on 28 February 1941, found the run into the new base somewhat confusing, but guessed that the delay was probably due to the reception party on land not having been fully prepared. Lehmann-Willenbrock had been awarded the Knight's Cross two days earlier, which meant there was going to be some high-powered welcome, with the Commander-in-Chief himself presenting the award. Despite arriving dead on time at the appointed

A wartime scene of a U-boat nosing towards the bunker at La Pallice.

The 105mm deck gun on the bows of U178 entering the lock at Bordeaux after a momentous voyage to the Far East. The bunkered lock, which was never completed, can be seen towards the right.

rendezvous, the radio severely blasted U96 for being half an hour early and told the men to wait until the proper appointed time. U46 left St Nazaire again on 15 March for a tragic voyage during which a Force 8 gale washed the first watch officer, Oblt.z.S. Helmut Pöttgen, overboard. He had temporarily unfastened his safety harness while on lookout duty and could not be recovered, despite a desperate search through the mountainous seas and high winds. Sadly this was not the first time this had happened to U46. Six months earlier, two men had disappeared overboard under similar conditions.

Despite a number of tragic events, the 7th U-Flotilla could boast of a vast number of Iron Crosses. No wonder the cream of the U-boat arm seems to have ended up under Sohler's care. The run of good luck came to an abrupt end with a rather unfortunate turn of events at around the time when the flotilla became fully operational in St Nazaire. Instead of resting on his laurels in the new base, Sohler had the unenviable task of writing some two hundred consolatory letters. U47 (Kptlt Günther Prien) U100 (Kptlt Joachim Schepke), U99 (Kptlt Otto Kretschmer) and U70 (Kptlt Joachim Matz) went down in rapid succession, at about the same time as the first boats were enjoying the high life in the new base. Sohler reacted by renaming his base 'Camp Prien' after the hero of Scapa Flow and the first naval Knight of the Iron Cross. At the same time, Sohler took it upon himself to adopt U47's emblem of a snorting bull for the entire flotilla with the nickname "The Snorting Bull Flotilla." Prien, Schepke, Kretschmer and Matz were perhaps the four best and most experienced U-Boat Commanders and this was a devastating run of losses.

Korvkpt. Klaus Scholtz, Chief of the 12th U-Flotilla based in Bordeaux, wearing the Knights Cross with Oakleaves around the neck and the Iron Cross First Class above the U-boat Badge on his left breast.

Viktor Schütze, Chief of the 2nd U-Flotilla in Lorient (who should not be confused with Herbert-Viktor Schütze of U605), at his desk. He is wearing the Knights Cross with Oakleaves around his neck.

At this time the flotilla looked as follows:

Flotilla Chief:	KK	Herbert Sohler
Adjutant:	OL	Ernst Krieg and later LT Karl Gabriel Gudenus
Secretary:	OL	Bachmeier
Kptlt. with the Staff:	KK	Freeden
Flotilla Administration Officer:	KL	Rüting
2nd Administration Officer:	OL	Christian Fuchs
3rd Administration Officer:	OL	Kunzke and later OL Behnke
Flotilla Engineering Officer:	KL	Sattler
2nd Engineering Officer:	OL	Röver
Transport Commander:	OL	Botsch
Chief Medical Officer:	MOSA	Dr. Rundte

Flotilla Registrar:	Oberschreibfeldwebel Hermann Schlicht
Registrar for Secret Matters:	Oberschreibfeldwebel Heinz Berthold
General Administration:	Stabsverwaltungsfeldwebel Kurt Krebs
Legal Matters:	Stabsoberfeldwebel Erich Badorreck
Flotilla Police Chief:	Bootsmann Kurt Weidner
Provisions Manager:	Oberverwaltungsfeldwebel Adolf Knöfel
Mechanical Office:	Stabsobermaschinist Willi Tyssen
Paramedic:	Medicalfeldwebel Hans Burmeister
Flotilla Navigator:	Obersteuermann Werner Carlsen
Flotilla Radio Operator:	Oberfunkmeister Erhard Konrad
Flotilla Torpedo Mechanic:	Obermechaniker Eugen Spadinger
Flotilla Artificer:	Oberfeuerwerker Karl Mandewirt
U-boat Provisions Office:	Oberverwaltungsfeldwebel Willi Meisner

The following U-boats were part of the 7th U-Flotilla:

U45, U46, U47, U48, U49, U50, U51, U52, U53, U54, U55, U69, U70, U71, U73, U74, U75, U76, U77, U88, U93, U94, U95, U96, U97, U98, U99, U100, U101, U102, U133, U135, U207, U213, U221, U224, U227, U255, U265, U266, U267, U274, U278, U281, U285, U300, U303, U310, U338, U342, U358, U359, U364, U381, U382, U387, U390, U397, U403, U406, U410, U427, U434, U436, U442, U448, U449, U453, U454, U455, U479, U481, U551, U552, U553, U567, U575, U576, U577, U578, U581, U593, U594, U602, U607, U617, U618, U624, U641, U647, U650, U662, U667, U678, U702, U704, U707, U710, U714, U751, U765, U962, U969, U974, U976, U980, U985, U988, U994, U1004, U1191, U1192, UA

A boat making its way into one of the wide, wet pens of the bunker at La Pallice.

Elbe II showing the inside of the western basin with three scuttled U-boats, all of them the latest Type XXI. After the war the Royal Navy recorded a considerable amount of clutter, but this particular area was completely free from anything, suggesting that what had been there was tipped into the water before the British army of occupation arrived. It seems highly probable that the boat nearest the quay on the left is U3506, the one in middle is U3004 and the one on the right U2505. For a long time after the war, these wrecks were well hidden inside a high security zone of the Howaldtswerke-Deutsche Werft, but when the shipyard vacated the site in the early 1990s, souvenir hunters found their way in to salvage whatever was left. The port authorities then filled the basin with sand.

The Brest bunker seen from the sea. Although the biggest building in the area, the huge concrete monstrosity is dwarfed by the hill behind with the naval school on the top. This entire area consists of hard rock, which has been hollowed out with tunnels leading to underground workshops, storerooms and fuel reservoirs.

2
Atlantic and Baltic Bases with U-boat Bunkers

NORWAY

Although sharing a long frontier with Sweden and forming an integral part of Scandinavia, Norway has a long tradition of being isolated and strongly independent. Probably because for part of the year this impressive country is ruled by the weather, which temporarily cuts it off from its neighbours and, at the same time, isolates individual communities within it. When Germany invaded in April 1940, Norway's strategic position with such a deeply incised coastline offered splendid opportunities for creating bases and anchorages for the Kriegsmarine. Being better

The making of Dora I in Trondheim, with part of the roof being put in place in the background. Once the walls were high and firm enough, it was possible to put the roof girders in place. Most of the metal visible in the distance was later covered with wooden shuttering to be hidden inside the solid, thick roof.

A close up of the cement being agitated while it settled into its mould. Seeing this, one immediately wonders how many men actually lost their concentration to fall into the slushy mix. Working high up, on cold and exposed timbers of the U-boat bunkers must have demanded not only a great deal of determination but also considerable physical and mental effort.

Everything was in short supply and teams of skilled workers toiled around the clock to produce the spare parts necessary to keep the complicated machinery running. Yet, despite this sophistication, large sections of the system functioned on makeshift wooden contrivances put up quickly to solve the daily problems. This shows the top end of the so-called 'ladder to heaven' where the pipes from the cement pumps stopped to regurgitate their contents onto the bunker.

located for reaching the Atlantic than far flung home ports, these provided an ideal springboard for challenging Britain, and the northerly fjords had the added attraction of being out of range of enemy land-based aircraft. U-boats started refuelling in Norway shortly after the Kriegsmarine had established itself there, but building up large shipyard facilities was considerably more difficult, and initially the Kriegsmarine could cope with only minor repairs. Many vessels were forced to return to German shipyards for more serious work. Of course, two months later, the strategic importance of Norway was somewhat overshadowed by Germany's gaining unfettered access to the French Atlantic coast.

The idea of building a supply and repair network in the north was voiced virtually before the invasion of Norway was complete and a number of fairly well prepared plans went ahead as soon as the political situation permitted. These centred around the old British concept of the submarine depot ship with repair and replenishment facilities on board. This method of operating had hardly been used in Germany, where flotilla escort ships served more as mobile headquarters and accommodation rather than workshops. A number of merchantmen made redundant by the war were fitted out as supply ships and moved into the well sheltered fjords of Norway to service Atlantic- and Arctic-bound U-boats. Although this worked very well, without a great deal of interruption from the British air force, the need for better protection was foreseen and for this purpose it was decided to build bunkers in both Trondheim and Bergen.

The first mentioned came under the jurisdiction of the Todt Organisation while the other project was to be undertaken by the German Naval Dockyard in Bergen. The Todt

Dora I in Trondheim showing the heavy portcullis type of armoured doors. Sliding down from the ceiling, these could shut off the space between the roof and water to prevent pressure waves from bursting bombs shattering the inside of the bunker.

Organisation leaned heavily on a firm from Frankfurt-am-Main, while a Munich-based contractor was chosen for Bergen. This was where the first problems occurred. Neither of them had a great deal of experience of foreign countries and they quickly found that conditions in Norway were totally different to what they had come to expect elsewhere. To start with, the insular nature of the country meant there was no army of unemployed itinerants queuing up for work. Therefore, instead of starting with several thousand helpers, the administrators had to contend with a few hundred, and often had to make do with less than half the required workforce. In addition to this, it must be borne in mind that the Arctic winters are exceedingly dark and cold, adding a considerable natural hurdle to any building venture.

Not only was there a shortage of labour, but the basic infrastructure for such a major construction programme was missing as well. The Norwegians built many of their houses out of timber with only a little stone, meaning that neither cement, sand nor hardcore played a significant role in the economy and the acquisition of these essential raw materials became a major problem. There were no local firms who could extract sand and hardcore in the required quantities from existing sources. There was also the problem of communications. Both roads and railways were often closed by ice and snow. In some cases, major reconstruction work was necessary because lines of communication were regularly washed down hillsides or swallowed up by soft ground when ice melted in spring. Even the sea did not provide a safe route. Bad weather delayed more ships than enemy action, and the transports had to contend with rocky shallows where the natural hazards usually won the battle. To make matters even worse, Norway was cut off from both Germany and Denmark by water, meaning that all transport routes involved a sea crossing, which added considerable delays to the journey times. It was not uncommon to take a delivery period of several weeks into account and many heavy items took up to four months, while a fair number of essential items were lost on the way.

Having sorted out the acquisition of building materials, it was necessary to import virtually all the specialised machinery as there was very little of it in Norway. This was not the end of the problem, though. Having organised the supply chain and recruited a labour force, it was soon realised that there were nothing like the empty schools of St Nazaire or the naval barracks in Brest to serve as emergency accommodation for the large numbers of temporary workers. So, living quarters had to be built from scratch, and the garden shed-type military huts used throughout Germany were hardly up to coping with the severe wintry conditions in the north. Having dealt with this problem too, kitchens, food stores, clothing stores, medical services and the like had to be organised. Whilst the Norwegians made no great effort to disrupt any of this, neither did they offer a great deal of assistance and many seemingly simple operations became major undertakings.

Work on Dora I in Trondheim started in 1941, shortly after Hitler had ordered Operation Barbarossa, the invasion of Soviet Russia. This conveniently provided a corps of prisoners of war for working on the bunker, and several hundred volunteers arrived, virtually fresh from the front, where they had been captured. The selection on the Russian steppes cannot have been terribly efficient because a large proportion of these

U433 under Oblt.z.S. Konstantin von Puttkamer with an almost transparent camouflage net thrown over the top.

U-boats in Danzig. Although out of reach of enemy aircraft, a camouflage covering has been added to hide the prominent, stark outlines of the submarines. This type of rigid structure was usually used by shipyards while the boat was still under construction so that men could work underneath it without being hampered by netting.

men suffered from such a variety of complaints that the staff in Trondheim considered them unfit for work. Consequently a sanatorium with adequate medical services was set up, where the Russians could recuperate.

The design of both Norwegian bunkers differed from those being erected in Germany and in France inasmuch as they were intended to have two floors, the lower one for mooring U-boats and an upper storey for accommodation, workshops and offices. However, by the end of the 1941, the building was already six months behind schedule and it looked as if the Trondheim project might never get off the ground. Consequently the plans for the upper floor were scrapped. The delay was due to the problems mentioned earlier, but the choice of site did not help. Although conveniently situated, it was at the end of a tidal fjord where a good deal of mud had accumulated over the millennia to produce a water saturated sediment, incapable of supporting the type of foundations used for other bunker projects. Underneath this were more problems in the form of alternating clay and sand layers, all likely to encourage water to seep through and flood the building site. Several ideas were tried to keep the groundwater at bay, but despite the special precautions many of the original schemes foundered, and in the end an expensive type of electrolysis was used. By passing an electrical current through the mud, it was found that sufficient water could be drained away to allow foundations to be sunk. Despite this ingenuity, especially large footings had to be laid, the upper parts of which are clearly visible in photographs. Instead of the walls resting on an underwater concrete raft or solid rock, large pontoon-type box foundations were put in to spread the weight. Since the tops of these served as walkways and quays, it is not always obvious that they are the result of especially troublesome substrata. Despite these precautions having been taken, Dora I settled considerably as more concrete was piled on top of the foundations. At first this amounted to a few centimetres, which was hardly visible to the untrained eye, but soon the subsidence increased to 15 centimetres, making it more difficult to hide. U-boat men weren't terribly concerned, but the sagging added a worrying dimension for the builders, who foresaw the development of cracks in both foundations and roof, although this did not happen.

Dora I was eventually handed over to the Kriegsmarine on 20 June 1943, by which time the second bunker in Trondheim, Dora II, had already been under construction for several months. Problems with machinery, supplies and labour continued to such an extent that it was hardly necessary for the Allies to disrupt the building process. The second bunker was little more than half completed by the time war ended. Although a number of U-boats withdrew to Norway at the end of the war, they did not have to endure much interference from Allied forces and the final end of the war came as a bit of an anticlimax for many. U-boat men lowered their flags for the last time. Some of them burned them and waited. Eventually the Royal Navy put in an appearance, checked that there were no scuttling charges on the U-boats, looted valuables from private lockers and then departed again. With the end of the war having been in sight for some time and the naval activities up there having been reduced considerably since the summer of 1944, a number of people were ordered out of Norway before the Allies could prevent their return to Germany.

The unfinished remains of the Dora I' bunker in Trondheim.

In Trondheim, the Germans closed the door to an underground hospital by the side of the bunker, but otherwise left things as they were. Even unused uniforms in the quartermaster's stores were left intact when the last remnants of the Kriegsmarine departed. Although relations with the local Norwegians had not been as cordial as the co-operation the Germans enjoyed in France, there been no great deal of open hostility either. For this reason many Germans did not feel the need to destroy what they were leaving behind. Some of the structures surfaced again as late as the mid-1980s when the area around the Trondheim bunkers was being developed for commercial use. Workmen discovered a rusty iron door behind a pile of timber and rubble, and on opening it found the labyrinth of an underground hospital put there to deal especially with wounded U-boat men. Being told to clear the site they could not be prevented from burning a number of crates containing Kriegsmarine uniforms, although one man, Knut Sivertsen, made a desperate effort to save the valuable historic artefacts. Today, parts of the unfinished bunker remain derelict, while the still functioning Dora I has been modified for commercial use. Indeed it has been undergoing a major facelift, with a new building being added around the outside of the old, drab concrete.

The Bergen project was started in a staccato fashion and the foundations there were hardly in place when the initial plans were modified to bring more services under cover of the one roof. It was decided to add accommodation space, storage areas and other facilities, although this did not distract too much from the plans for building a couple of

The Elbe II bunker in Hamburg shortly before the end of the war with curtain, rather than portcullis, type of armoured doors sealing off the two boat entrances. The buildings on the roof were put there to overcome an acute shortage of space. The building towards the left, attached to the side of the bunker was a staircase, added to the outside to enable staff to get easily into the buildings on the roof. This was not bombproof and has since disappeared. The buildings along the bottom were also demolished, but quickly replaced by huts to provide additional office and administration space for the shipyard.

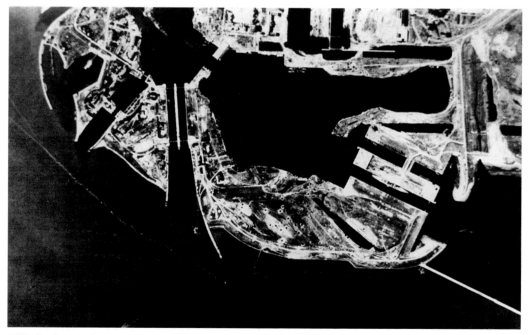

Wilhelmshaven showing the floating harbour with the various sealocks.

Peering down the so-called 'ladder to heaven' from the roof of the bunker at Bordeaux. Although rickety looking, these structures had to carry considerable weight and be wide enough for a good number of men to undo the joints when the pipes clogged. The building in the background housed both cement mixers and pumps. Bad weather was a special problem during northern winters, when there was a tendency for water to freeze in the pipes.

Personnel bunkers built of concrete and brick were common throughout German towns during the Second World War. The majority were demolished after the war, but this one survived because such activity could also have damaged the underground and houses towards the right. The high-water defence wall on the left was not built until the mid-1960s and during the war there was direct access to the river. Although the bunker has survived, the Federal German government is wary of symbols like the swastika, which has been removed from the base of the eagle above the door.

A similar type of personnel bunker in Wilhelmshaven, built with reinforced concrete. Behind it are naval quarters and offices.

additional floors on top of the U-boat berths. This almost windowless layer gave the impression of there being an incredibly thick roof, looking somewhat like a more modern, enclosed multi-storey car park. It was decided to take advantage of the plentiful supply of granite in the area by placing huge blocks, about a cubic metre in size, on top of the roof as an additional layer for repelling bombs. Later, as the building got underway, it became apparent that this proposition was somewhat of a necessity because there was not enough cement ever to stick these blocks in place. Instead, the spaces between individual stones were filled in with sand and a only a thin layer of cement was used around the edges to prevent this from being washed out by the incessant weather. 1945 was hardly under way when 617 Squadron RAF attacked the bunker with two dozen or so Tallboys, two of which hit the bunker to blast funnel shaped holes in the roof. This clearly demonstrated the effectiveness of the double ceiling construction by preventing the rubble from dropping down on to the U-boats below. Instead, the majority of loose material collected on the floor above. However, the blasts were sufficient to knock a number of supporting walls out of true and, as had been the case with other construction sites, the near-misses created utter havoc with machinery outside. This was so bad that work was halted so that virtually all the energies of the labour force could be directed towards clearing the damage, and this was still going on when the war ended.

The bunker was bombed before the roof was completed and before the armoured doors for the individual pens could be delivered. Some of the internal walls were blasted out of true, making further construction work pointless until the major flaw could be rectified. In the end, the Germans decided the problem could not be put right before the end of hostilities and the bunker was abandoned. After the war it wasn't much use, either to the Norwegians nor the Allies, and consequently the whole structure was demolished. Being as obstinate as some of its German counterparts, not all of it fell down. Although much was reduced to rubble, three of the north-easterly pens remained intact and can still be seen.

KIEL

On maps it looks as if the city of Kiel is situated at the end of a long estuary, but closer examination will reveal that there is no river, other than the small Schwentine running into the side of this massive inlet. There are a number of such deep indentations along the Baltic coast, all fairly similar to Norwegian fjords but lacking the steep sided surrounding hills. These features also bear some resemblance to the drowned valleys of Devon and Cornwall on England's south coast. The water in them is salty and tends to be fairly deep, often with plenty of jellyfish in summer. The Germans call this type of deep indentation of the sea 'Förde' and since there is no English equivalent, we will use the same term.

The Kiel Förde is about eight kilometres deep and a good kilometre wide with a narrow stretch near the mouth, making it such an ideal anchorage that the city owes its rapid growth entirely to the presence of the navy. This hive of naval activity has helped to make Kiel not only the largest town in Schleswig-Holstein, but also the seat of the

The rather long Kilian bunker in Kiel seen from the side, shortly after the end of the war. The town of Kiel, the saltwater Förde and the boat entrances lie towards the left, while the small boat is making its way up the Schwentine river to the right. The section of the bunker containing heavy workshops can just be made out towards the right of the photograph. The top of the accommodation and office block sticks up beyond the roof towards the middle while a raised anti-aircraft platform is visible towards the left.

provincial government, which has been there since a few years before the First World War. Being landlocked and without a tide makes the Förde an ideal natural harbour and the strong naval presence, as well as the difficulty of expanding sideways owing to the relatively high ground, meant that the commercial side of the port never developed beyond the limited needs of the local community. Most of the Baltic trade passed through Lübeck, Stettin and other ports to the east. Strong northerly to easterly winds tend to raise the water level in the Förde by up to 1.5 metres, while a southerly will lower it by up to one metre. But this gradual process of extremes is hardly noticeable and for most of the time there is no significant change in water level.

By the time the Second World War started, there was a vast range of naval facilities in the Förde, from dockyard, arsenal and pressure dock for submarines to supply depots of all kinds. The famous Krupp Germania works, which built U-boats during both world wars, was located as far inland as the Förde stretches. Being opposite the railway station, with easy access to the waterside, meant one could obtain good views of what was going on, although many operations were hidden behind tarpaulins and, later by security gates in front of large hangar-like buildings. In addition to this, there was also Howaldswerke on the eastern side of the Förde, next to the naval arsenal and, before the war, Deutsche Werke occupied what is now HDW (Howaldswerke–Deutsche Werft) and the naval arsenal.

Not only did the names of these shipbuilders change after the war, but many of the naval installations along that eastern side were re-landscaped to produce a totally different shoreline. For example, the heavy cruiser (and earlier pocket battleship) *Admiral Scheer* capsized in one of the basins and was then buried under rubble from the ruins of Kiel. At the same time another large port basin was also filled in. Today it is exceedingly difficult to find any signs from the war along this shore, but sufficient landmarks remain in the town on the western side to reccgnise the skyline from old photographs. However, there is still ample naval and shipbuilding activity and anyone taking a ferry ride from the main railway station out towards the sea will be rewarded with a plethora of interesting sights. It is also worth considering a *Hafenrundfahrt* or Dock Tour by boat, which takes passengers from Kiel to Laboe and passes closer to the port installations than regular ferries.

Kilian and Konrad bunkers, built from 1941–3 and 1943–4 respectively, were two totally different structures. Kilian was built in the water immediately to the north of the small Schwentine river. It was intended to be used for finishing off new boats rather than as a docking base for operational ones. The reason being that there was ample deep water on the far side of the Förde from the naval dockyard and the Kriegsmarine developed the cheaper practice of sending boats with skeleton crews over there, to be laid on the seabed, in order to escape the incessant air raids on the city. Kilian differed from the other bunkers by having a couple of relatively small entrances but being some 150 metres long. Only just over 10 metres of this distance was taken up with protective gates at the front and there were workshops at the opposite, landward end; but, despite this, there was still sufficient length for two Type VII boats to fit in, one behind the other, and the pens were wide enough to accommodate a total of 12 such boats. Towards the end of the war, even longer boats were put inside, with either their bows or sterns protruding out beyond the gates.

The armoured entrances were something of an enigma. Made up of 3 metre wide sliding sections, they covered the area from the ceiling to the water, but there was no

Before the war, and later in Norwegian fjords out of reach of aircraft based in Britain, it was common for boats to cluster around a depot ship. This shows the Weichsel *in the Baltic with school boats lying alongside. The camouflage pattern would suggest that the photograph was taken after the beginning of the war, probably somewhere in the eastern Baltic.*

protection lower down. At first glance this seems to be insignificant, but the designers must have known that the city on the opposite shore was likely to attract bombs and consequently a good number would probably explode in the water, creating episodic waves which would wash across the Förde and into the bunker. As has already been mentioned, one boat, U4708, a Type XXIII under Oblt.z.S. Dietrich Schultz, was sunk in the bunker a few days before it was due to have been commissioned.

With the bunker being stuck out from the shore, the designers had to sacrifice a railway connection and the only access from the landward side was by lorry. As well as space for submarines, there was an accommodation and administration block by the side, but the walls of this were less than half a metre thick, giving the occupants limited protection. There was also an anti-aircraft battery on the top. As with so many other bunkers, Kilian survived the war to be demolished by British Royal Engineers afterwards.

The other bunker, Konrad, differed inasmuch that it was built on top of an existing dry dock, which had been in commission since the end of the nineteenth century. Like Kilian, it was intended as a finishing-off bunker, rather than moorings for operational boats, and it was later used for building midget submarines. Although the navy had planned to put the bunker directly on the dry dock apron, none of the building firms were terribly keen on this idea, saying they could not guarantee that the foundations would carry the additional weight. There was a strong chance that the main basin might crack, which would then create more problems by allowing water to seep in from the underlying layers of sand and gravel. In view of this, foundations were excavated to a depth of almost eight metres. This was done quite simply by flooding the dock, pushing barges in and then emptying the spoil into them for removal out to sea.

The building process had hardly got under way when drastic changes in the general scenario of the war suggested that modifications were called for. The most noteworthy of these was to extend the length of the dry dock to make the structure stick out almost 30 metres into the basin in front of the gate. Extending in the other direction was not practical due to existing buildings and shortage of space. Much of the quay area was built up with industrial plant of one kind and another and these sheds were hemmed in dramatically by a constricting ring of high-rise flats for dockyard workers. This acute shortage of space became even more of a problem after the war, when it was decided to fill in the entire basin to create more space for construction. Eventually, some years after the war, a number of welding sheds were built on top of this site.

The shortage of space was a major hurdle while building the Konrad bunker and another dry dock on the western side was filled in to serve as a base for the cement mixers. Some of the walls, built as floatable concrete boxes, had to be moulded in the old locks of the Kiel Canal at Holtenau, several kilometres away, and floated over. There were two sets of locks there because the first were completed before the First World War, shortly before the appearance of the Dreadnought battleship, which was too big to fit through. Therefore the widening of the canal and the construction of bigger locks started shortly after the official opening by Kaiser Wilhelm II.

Konrad's location close to several major dockyards as well as the centre of the town meant that it was a problem to get it completed because the work was so often

U123 lying next to the Tirpitz Pier in Kiel, with an accommodation ship on the far side of the screen, protecting U-boats from view. The net cutter would suggest that this photograph was taken early on in the war. The boat had three different commanders. The first was Kptlt Karl-Heinz Moehle, who later became chief of the 5th U-Flotilla, the second, Kptlt Reinhard Hardegen who led the first attack (Operation Paukenschlag) against the United States and the third was Horst von Schroeter. All three were Knights of the Iron Cross.

interrupted by air raids. The worst damage to the bunker itself occurred when a 50cm deep hole was blown in the roof, but the surrounding cement mixers and concrete pumps suffered worse by being put out of action. At first the machinery was repaired or replaced but eventually the raids were so intensive that the building process often came to a standstill and work stopped for several weeks at a time. Air raids were not the only cause of delay. Like Valentin, the Konrad project suffered from a general shortage of everything and workers were often left sitting around to pass the time while they waited for material to be delivered.

Konrad had hardly been completed, when it was decided instead to use it for building midget submarines of the Seehund type. A number of photographs have appeared in books showing these being assembled on a production line basis inside the hangar-like building. Although hardly ever identified, these photos in fact show bunker Konrad in Kiel. As has already been said, the bunker was demolished after the war, the site filled with rubble from ruins and new buildings erected on top. The area is within a shipyard security zone, making access difficult and somewhat pointless because virtually nothing is left there to indicate the war had ever taken place.

Part of the inside wall of the Kilian bunker in Kiel. It seems quite likely that the top part of this inscription is authentic, although the bottom part could well have been added after the war, perhaps as part of a film set. Either the Third Reich issued a good number of identical stencils and the same colour paint or the words were a postwar addition.

This notice on what was once the back wall of the Kilian bunker in Kiel is probably authentic. Having been shielded from both light and weather the paint is in reasonably good condition.

The Kilian bunker was blown up most dramatically immediately after the war, bringing down most of the roof and leaving a twisted mass of concrete. Being situated in a more out of the way location, by the side of a wide part of the Förde, meant that the demolished remains were left in peace until the late 1970s when renewed attempts were made to remove what the local newspaper described as an eyesore.

There is a ruling saying that the removal of war remains containing explosives will be paid for by the Federal German Government, however city councils must foot the bill if there are no explosives present. It would appear that an attempt was made to explore the Kilian ruin during the late 1970s with the view of possibly locating some gunpowder so that the German taxpayer rather than the local ratepayer would see to the highly expensive bill of removing the ruin. This was not as easy as it sounds because much of the roof was brought down during the demolition, leaving several metres of concrete on top of whatever had once been inside. Getting access to the interior was indeed a major problem, but a diving team did manage to find a small opening, only just big enough for a camera to be inserted, and thereby proved that U4708 was indeed still lying under the rubble. Newspaper coverage then resulted in several people coming forward saying that they had relatives entombed in the remains. Research revealed that the bunker had not been thoroughly searched before demolition took place and there was also a strong possibility of live torpedoes as well as other ammunition lying deep down among the rubble. In addition to this there was the strong suggestion that both torpedoes and other ammunition were hurled some distance out into the deep waters of the Förde, where a number of large ferries to Scandinavia pass each day.

The major snag with the location of possible explosives was that the base of the bunker ruins was covered in fine silt to a depth of about two metres, making it difficult to establish what actually is there. There was no resistance when the divers touched the surface of the silt and it would have been a relatively easy matter to pump it out, but at this stage environmentalists put their oar in, warning that the deposit could contain all manner of dangerous waste including heavy metals and other poisons. This meant that it was no longer possible to pump the sediment out and dump it at sea. Instead, the sludge became a political football of immense proportions. On the one side were the people who wanted the bunker to remain as a war grave and on the other was heavy money, which required the site for redevelopment. Newspaper reports of the time tended to reflect a general ignorance of history, making it difficult to separate fact from fiction, but it would appear that the problem was shelved by declaring the remains a listed monument. The local authority even went as far as to illuminate it at night. Unfortunately, as is often the case, emotional considerations take second place to the power of money and the value of the site increased to such extent that, by the year 2000, the bunker had been closed off and the site was being filled in with sand. It appears that the ruins are going to be levelled so that a new development can be placed on the top and, at the time of writing, it looks as if these poignant remains of the war are about to vanish from sight. It is certainly possible that nothing will be left by the time this book is published.

HAMBURG

Until about a hundred years ago, the river Elbe divided into a myriad of channels upstream from Hamburg to create a delta-like mass of islands within a huge basin some eight kilometres wide. Some of these islets were stable enough to support trees, while others were nothing more than semi-permanent sandbanks which were washed away during periods of exceptionally high water. Reputed to have harboured a number of undesirables who had run away from justice in the city, they were used for grazing sheep during the dry summer months when they could be reached by boat. At the beginning of the last century, when the coming of steam created a rapid increase in the demand for port facilities, a number of shipbuilders crossed over the half-kilometre-wide northern branch of the Elbe to establish their businesses on the islands to the south of an already thriving seaport. This rapid expansion was very much supported by the city fathers, and the State

Some of the bunkers cum flaktowers built in towns to protect civilians were even larger than the U-boat bunkers. This shows the bunker near Feld Strasse in Hamburg. The windows were a post-war addition.

This dead-end roadway used to lead down to a floating dry dock. When this photo was taken in April 2000, this once busy centre for shipbuilding was in the process of being dried out to be converted into a new container terminal. The bunker has since been demolished and the ground level raised by several metres. The partly collapsed section of the eastern pen is clearly visible and so is the top of the wall which protects ships from the sharp concrete remains lying in the water. The far quay, which was used by the salvage firm Harms, has now been converted into a container port.

contributed by building a tunnel under the river to reach this new hive of activity. Building on those still wild islands was a relatively simple affair. All that needed to be done was to create some form of shuttering to prevent erosion and then to fill up the space behind with a plentiful supply of sand pumped out of the river itself. The initial foundations for the new quays were nothing more than oak trees pushed into the ground with warehouses built on top. This tried method had been used in old Hamburg for centuries and worked exceedingly well to create one of the biggest ports in Europe.

This man-made network of rivers and canals remained fairly stable until 1962, when a combination of circumstances wrought havoc by flooding the entire area from Hamburg town hall right across to the southern hills more than 14 kilometres away. The Hamburg waterfront has always been used to occasional flooding by exceptionally high tides, but this was more than expected. It was caused by unusually large quantities of water flowing down the river while a strong north-westerly gale prevented the high tide from emptying out into the North Sea. Consequently, the second high tide was blown in on top of an already alarmingly high water level. The results were disastrous. The suburb of Wilhelmsburg disappeared completely under the deluge and many people drowned. As a result, river defences were not only strengthened but also modified to take on their present shape and this realignment of major river systems has made it very difficult to track down the centres of activity during the two world wars, especially the location

The attempts to demolish air raid shelters after the war left the Allies with considerable embarrassment and, despite a shortage of everything, some Germans sacrificed valuable paint to write the slogan 'Made in Germany' on the walls after a number of concerted efforts failed to bring the bunkers down. Unable to demolish some of the bunkers with explosives, British soldiers satisfied themselves by blowing out the staircases in the interior, preventing masses of homeless refugees from sheltering in them from the exceptionally harsh winters immediately after the war.

Not all bunkers were used for long after the war and some of them remain as empty shells to this day. This shows the flak-tower-cum-air raid shelter in Wilhelmsburg, only a couple of kilometres from the Elbe II submarine pens in the Vulkanhafen. Considerable efforts have been made to hide it by planting trees around the outside and allowing vegetation to grow on the upper platform.

Looking across the 600 metre-wide northern Elbe from Teufelsbrück by the side of Jenisch Park to what was Deutsche Werft. The Fink II bunker was situated a short distance towards the right, but faced away from the river to be camouflaged by piers and buildings and was therefore difficult to spot from this side. Most of this site has now been levelled and re-landscaped, leaving virtually nothing of what was once one of the biggest shipyards in Hamburg. The cube-like office block, towards the left of the two ships on the stocks, and dwarfed by the gantry crane system, is still standing, but it is now overshadowed by a much taller building.

The interior of Elbe II, looking out into the Vulkanhafen at low tide to reveal the presence of U2501, a fourth Type XXI, scuttled in front of the bunker. The majority of armoured doors can be seen stacked neatly towards the left of the opening, but one section has come adrift from the others to hang at a precarious angle from the ceiling.

where Fink II, the U-boat pen, once stood. (It might be interesting to add that Bernhard Rogge, the wartime commander of the legendary raider *Atlantis*, was the officer in charge of the Federal Armed Forces which did such a fantastic job of carrying out rescue work during those floods of 1962.)

Fink II was built in a somewhat underpopulated part of what was then still an island reached from the rest of the docks by ferry. There was also a single railway bridge and one narrow road bridge carrying nothing more than a cobblestoned country lane. The 250 metre-wide channel of the Southern Elbe separated it from the marshy mainland on the south and the busy half a kilometre-wide Northern Elbe from the suburbs of Hamburg. Deutsche Werft had established itself there shortly after the First World War and co-existed with a tiny community of fishermen and fruit farmers. The majority of workers were brought over from the city by barge. Indeed, a large proportion of the port's labour force was ferried over from the city's underground stations on the northern side by a mass of small boats especially employed for the purpose. Fink II was built on dry ground, some hundred metres or so from the side of a canal branching directly off the river Elbe. Once ready for occupation, the old shuttering along the edge of the canal was removed and a large triangular patch of land was washed out to totally change the shape of the area. After the war an airfield was built on the western extremities of the Finkenwerder island and this has recently been enlarged by filling in another canal close to the one on which the bunker used to be located. So the outline of the shore there has changed a number of times in the last sixty years or so.

Being far from habitable housing, Fink II was demolished after the war with a large stock of old Luftwaffe bombs and then covered with sand pumped out of the river. This effort produced an incredibly loud bang with a cloud like an atomic bomb mushrooming high into the sky, but it did comparatively little damage. Blowing a few of the internal walls out of true, the roof was brought down over three of the five pens, but none of the ceilings showed any signs of cracking. Instead, they remained perched at precarious angles until workers with pneumatic drills and heavy breaking gear set to. It seems highly likely that this demolition effort was part of a grand British deception plan, to impress upon the Russians and the rest of the world the accuracy of the Royal Air Force's bombing campaign. Pictures of the remains have appeared with captions saying it was the result of the special bombs developed by Britain towards the end of the war. Yet there was very little visible damage when the war ended and all five pens were still standing defiantly, having resisted Barnes Wallis's heavy earthquake bombs.

The process of covering the bunker site with sand once more changed the appearance of the shoreline, making it not the easiest of tasks to find the spot where the bunker was buried, and all that remains visible today is a huge mound. To make matters worse, Deutsche Werft was one of the first concerns to fail as a result of the shipbuilding industry's decline in Europe and the yard closed during the mid-1960s. Most of the industrial remains were demolished and the site then completely re-landscaped. To make recognition of the old shorelines more difficult still, the mouth of the Southern Elbe was blocked off shortly after the disastrous flood and a new road built to carry heavy commuter traffic from new outlying residential areas to run along a by-pass around the old Finkenwerder High Street. New industries centred on yachting were built on the land which had once been Deutsche Werft and there is little left to suggest that this parkland area was once a busy shipyard. The old administrative building is still standing and one can just about find a small number of relics left over from the slipways. On top of this there are a few pieces of evidence, such as a bunch of high-tension electricity cables, indicating a possibly industrial past. Yet, anyone seeking evidence of a U-boat bunker is going to be disappointed. Great care has been taken to hide any suggestion that there was one, once.

Originally, the designs for both bunkers in Hamburg were fairly similar, although their foundations differed considerably. Fink II in Finkenwerder was enlarged from a two pen to a massive five pen affair, capable of holding fifteen U-boats. The first bunker, Elbe II, built into the waters of the Vulkanhafen, had sufficient space for adding another half a dozen or so pens by the side but this extension was never started. The name of the basin is an interesting relic from early times, when the Vulkan Works of Stettin established a thriving yard for building fast steamships and First World War submarines in Hamburg. Although the firm remained as one of Germany's major shipbuilders until the end of the Second World War, its activities in Hamburg fizzled out during the depression of the 1920s and the site was taken over by Howaldtswerke. Elbe II was put up as a fitting-out bunker for U-boats built by this firm, also by Blohm und Voss, Germany's largest private shipbuilders, who had their main base at the entrance to the dock basin. The word Vulkan fell foul of language reforms at the beginning of the twentieth century when the letter 'c' with a 'k' sound was changed to 'k', for which reason one still finds both spellings in proper nouns, while during the Second World War there was the Vulkan Works in Bremen and the older Vulkan Yard in Stettin. It may also be interesting to add that Professor Hellmuth Walter, who designed the revolutionary high-speed U-boats, started his astonishing career at the Vulkan Works in Hamburg and worked for several years very close to the site where Elbe II was later built.

Elbe II was constructed by driving piles into the river bed and then building the bunker on top. At the same time, the numerous office and administrative buildings surrounding this site were made more durable by having bombproof wings added. Other buildings had their cellars strengthened by incorporating old railway tracks under the ceilings so that the basements could be used as air raid shelters. It was thought that the strengthened ceilings would hold up a collapsed building until the unfortunate victims below found a way out. In addition to this, cellar windows were covered from the outside with concrete blocks measuring about 50 cm by 50 cm and a metre or so long. This was roughly the maximum size workers could manhandle into place without a crane. There were not many cellars in this part of the docks, because exceptionally high water tended to flood them at least once or twice a year, making their use somewhat limited. The Vulkanhafen site had a number of disadvantages, the biggest being the shortage of space; even the bunker roof had workshops and administrative buildings perched on top. This was partly designed as a camouflage aid to confusing attacking aircraft, but also to alleviate the acute shortage of office space.

Removing Elbe II after the war presented considerably more problems than blowing up Fink II, since there was a very real danger of destroying nearby buildings. Three firms went bankrupt trying to remove the remains of the Elbe II bunker, and despite a considerable effort involving a lot of explosives placed in appropriate places, much of the structure remained. In the end the site was cordoned off and, although the bunker remained in sight, people simply tried to pretend that it was not there. This was not terribly difficult, since it was in an out-of-the-way location, a few metres within the boundaries of the freeport.

The freeport is still today surrounded by a high fence but, immediately after the war, it was also protected by armed guards. The only way in and out was through a limited number of recognised checkpoints, with impressive barriers across the roads and manned by meticulous customs officers, the reason being that it was not necessary to pay duty on imports until they were taken out of the port. So, in a way the entire area can be looked upon as one massive bonded warehouse, where there was a plentiful supply of food that did not exist on the other side of the fence. The public was prevented from entering, workers needed passes and official visitors required written permission. Although these rules were relaxed during the 1950s, there was still very little general public traffic passing through the freeport. That is not to say that those who worked there bowed to their new masters, but a flourishing smuggling trade was organised to bring out food, which was in such desperately short supply immediately after the war. The army of occupation required German civilians to live for a couple of years on fewer calories than those allowed earlier to concentration camp inmates and, with people dying of starvation, encouraged a number of port workers to smuggle considerable quantities. Part of this fence close to the Elbe II bunker is made up from old anti-submarine and anti-torpedo netting, perhaps the last remains of the boom which used to protect the river near Cuxhaven.

In addition to being in the freeport, the ruins of the Elbe II were also within a tight security zone of the HDW's (Howaldtswerke–Deutsche Werft – HDW) sphere of operations. Being fenced off from the freeport meant that the only way into the bunker was past another, well-guarded entrance. Even with permission to visit the ruins, it was necessary to leave one's identity card or passport with the gatekeepers and special authority to carry a camera was given only on the understanding that no effort would be made to photograph the shipyard's operations. So, for many years Elbe II was in a high security area.

Shortly before Christmas 1984, however, the Royal Navy's Submarine Museum at HMS *Dolphin* in Gosport was asked to help with the identification of a U-boat in the bunker. It appeared that a British soldier guarding the site towards the end of 1948 had spent some time unscrewing a sighting compass from a submarine inside the ruins. This 'confession' was somewhat surprising at the time. Reliable records stated that all U-boats had been sunk during Operation Deadlight and virtually none remained, except a small number which were commissioned into some Allied navies at the end of the war. I had known the site since childhood and remembered the mass of concrete blocking the entrance. This suggested that anything which was in there in 1948 was still going to be there in 1984. An investigative letter to HDW produced a fascinating invitation to inspect the bunker at low tide. Yet reaching it was a major problem. Indeed, trying to get there without a car is still not the easiest of undertakings. Public transport within the port was restricted to ferrying workers to and from their places of employment at shift changes, not for taking casual visitors to critical places at low tide. The opportunity of possibly finding three U-boats lured Wolfgang Hirschfeld, the distinguished historian, author and ex-U-boat radio operator with his car to Hamburg and, together, we set off to inspect the ruins. In those days, during the summer of 1985, it was also possible to reach the bunker by ferry, but when this was not running it entailed a six kilometre walk.

Herr Traband, our guide from HDW, had known the site since the war and told us that nothing had changed a great deal. The U-boats were still lying where they had been scuttled all those years earlier. Sadly, the engines and conning towers of two boats had been removed during that drastic demolition process, but the rusting hulks under the sloping roof were easily recognisable as Type XXI U-boats. Although Howaldtswerke–

Deutsche Werft had known about them all along, the fact of their existence had hardly ever been allowed to trickle out and our accidental 'discovery' produced some intriguing responses. Many people didn't believe us, even after they had seen photographic evidence; and then, when others took the trouble to verify the 'find', some groups battled for the credit of having done the research which led to the rediscovery. Indeed it was quickly heralded on the other side of the Atlantic as an American achievement!

Shortly before I visited the site for the first time, a metre-high pile of papers arrived at HMS *Dolphin* where I was researching. Curious to see what this recent release contained, I started to pull out some sheets about halfway up because they were the only ones sticking out at an untidy angle. Imagine my surprise when this turned out to be a report by Lt Cmdr W.N. Eade about the condition of the dock facilities around the Elbe II bunker. From his report it was possible to identify the boats as U3506, U3004 and U2505. U2501 was scuttled outside the bunker and had been removed shortly after the end of the war.

Many things changed during the last fifteen years of the twentieth century. HDW withdrew its operations from Hamburg and that security fence which had kept sightseers at bay for so long was taken down. At the same time, a number of newspaper and magazine articles described the unusual occupants of the ruin and relic hunters made their way into the bunker to salvage whatever could be removed. In the end, the authorities pumped the place full of sand to deter visiting scavengers. However, they did not calculate on the cunning of these souvenir traders. Apparently some people had measured the position of the open hatches before the sand was pumped in and then dug down to them to remove further items from the insides of the boats. This in itself was quite a delicate undertaking because on most days the tide did not go down far enough to allow access to the interior. On top of this, one must not imagine the bunker as being flooded with nice clean water. At low tide it looked like black sludge, so thick that it closely resembled used motor oil rather than water. And the day when we were there in 1985, the scurrying of rats made it easier for us to obey HDW's request not to climb down the rusty ladders in case they broke off. Incidentally, great credit must go to Hamburg's conservation projects, which have been responsible for cleaning up these waters. They are now so clean that they harbour a wide variety of wildlife.

In 1985, there were still a dozen or more armoured portable sentry boxes littered around the area. Half a dozen or so had been stored by the side of the bunker, but there were also a few more by the side of the little-used railway tracks. In 2000 only a couple remained, although the bunker has not changed much since HDW vacated the site. There are notices telling people to keep out because there is a danger of the structure falling down, but it seems highly unlikely that it will do that in the lifetime of even the youngest visitor. The original doorways are fenced off with substantial netting, but peering in one can see a number of well-trodden paths to suggest that there have been numerous intruders who either cannot read or have disregarded the notice telling them to keep out. Today, the bunker is surrounded by a container depot, with massive boxes stacked even higher than the ruin, but finding it is not terribly difficult and until the year 2000 there appeared to be no restrictions on walking round part of the outside. A roadway leading up to the bunker certainly provided good enough access to get a good view of the structure. There were no notices or barriers preventing one from taking a curious peep into Germany's turbulent past.

Unlike many of its British counterparts, the old Hamburg docks are not yet totally redundant and this part, like so many other areas of the freeport, is in the process of being re-landscaped. Almost the entire Vulkan basin has been cut off from the main waterway with steel shuttering and is slowly being filled with sand. In September 2000, at low tide, it looked very much like a beach, with the ground apparently solid enough to walk over. This filling-in process is planned to continue, to make way for a new container port, until the new level reaches two metres above normal high tide. The idea being to keep the area dry even when the low land floods as a result of exceptionally high water. This means that most of the bunker is going to be hidden. And with so little of the ruin sticking out, it seems highly likely that builders will find a way of also covering the few pieces of protruding concrete, to use the site for some profitable purpose. It could well be that the last remains of the Elbe II will also disappear from sight during the early years of the twenty-first century.

BREMEN

The bunker building programme in Hamburg, Bremen, Wilhelmshaven and Kiel appears to have advanced on an ad hoc basis and it may be difficult to understand some of the decisions taken. For example, the first bunker to be built in Bremen was started in 1943, almost four years after the beginning of the war, while work had already started in Hamburg during 1940 and in Kiel in 1941. On the other hand, U-boat construction had returned to Bremen in 1935 when U25 was laid down at Deschimag AG Weser on 28 June, while the first post-First World War U-boat was not started in Hamburg until after the beginning of the Second World War, on 21 November 1939, when U551 was laid down at Blohm und Voss. And Kiel can claim even stronger and earlier connections with submarine construction than Bremen. Although Wilhelmshaven was the major naval base for the North Sea, a bunker for accommodating U-boats was planned but never built there. The main reason for this sequence appears to have been the availability of suitable space for the massive construction sites.

Bremen is situated some distance inland, on the banks of the river Weser, which is probably more famous for the story of the Pied Piper of Hamelin. When the development of steam forced a rapid increase in the demand for bigger and better port installations, Bremen was at a considerable disadvantage in not having suitable land for expanding into Consequently, a new port, then known as Wesermünde and now called Bremerhaven, grew up on the estuary of the river Weser. Although this blossomed into a substantial harbour in its own right, the shipbuilding industry remained firmly entrenched in the old city, probably because that supplied the massive specialist labour force.

The first bunker to be built here, Hornisse, was put up on top of an almost completed construction lock by the side of the river, in a tidal part of the harbour. The geology of

The Hornisse bunker in Bremen with a modern office block built directly on top of the roof. The river Weser is on the other side of the bunker, but a good way down, therefore the roof appears to be relatively low and has easily been concealed behind a number of modern buildings. Although this opening at the back appears to be a vast span, there are another two supporting walls in the deep shadows of the middle, where two buttresses can just be seen sticking out from under the lintel. The bunker was built on top of a dry dock and the workshops at the back have never been completed, nor has the front part of the massive structure.

The centre wall, supporting the heavy roof, runs along the full length of what was once a dry dock.

that area consists of sand and clay mixtures but even the clays are not solid. Instead, they are interlaced with a good number of sand-filled arteries, which act as drainage channels. Being deep underground means that water pressure in them can be quite considerable. This is still such a problem in some places that holes in the ground quickly fill up with water and in towns it is often prohibited to keep pumps running at night with a view to keeping excavations dry when no one is working in them, the reason being that the removal of too much water could lead to settlement cracks in nearby houses. Many buildings on this type of substrate have special cellars which function like the hull of a boat. That is, the foundations prevent water from seeping into the basement and at the same time, allow the building to almost float in the water-soaked ground during periods of heavy rainfall. To overcome this difficulty, the new dry dock being built at Deschimag AG Weser had a four-metre-thick base to act as a raft and thereby prevent one part from settling more than another. More supports were later sunk by its side to take the additional weight of the walls and roof for the new bunker.

Having originally been designed for large ships, meant the bunker was long enough to hold one submarine behind another. However, the massive width could not be roofed by a single span and it was necessary to built a dividing wall lengthways down the middle. This was not a great problem because there was still sufficient width in each pen to hold two submarines side by side. The roof differed from many of the other bunkers by having the wet cement supported by reinforced concrete arched beams rather than iron girders. The bunker, however, was never finished. The back portion was in place towards

The inside of the Hornisse bunker in Bremen showing the centre wall and the low water level of the river Weser. This is tidal and the dark green algae of the high water mark can be made out against the lighter coloured concrete. The walls look rather thin, but there were two of them, side by side with a narrow gap in between.

Although the Valentin bunker is almost half a kilometre long, it is not terribly wide, as can be seen here on what was the river or exit side of the production line for Type XXI U-boats. Much of the building has been hidden behind a thick layer of trees. The damage to the roof was done after the war when the bunker was used as a target for bombing trials.

the end of March 1945 when a major air raid disrupted proceedings. The bunker itself was hardly damaged, but heavy cranes, cement mixers and the all important pumps were destroyed beyond use and no great effort was made to replace them.

I first found the bunker by accident while looking for the remains of the Deschimag AG Weser ship yard and had no problems looking around without an appointment. Men working at the back had no objections to me taking photographs. The back wall had either not been built or had been removed again, making it possible to get a good view of the interior. Getting into it without a boat would be a major problem because there are no walkways or quays under the roof.

The shipbuilding part of the tidal harbour by the side of the river Weser has changed dramatically during the last years of the twentieth century, as a result of Deschimag AG Weser ceasing operations. In 1999, much of the site was being demolished to make way for new development and only some of the old machine shops, away from the quays, were still being used commercially. The old roads, complete with their original cobblestones, and the railways looked the same as they did during the war, but by the time this book is published, they will probably have changed beyond recognition. The turmoil of the new development will, no doubt, continue for a good while before the area settles down in its new role. Yet this should not put off anyone searching for historic remains in this part of Bremen. There is sufficient evidence to give a reasonable picture of what was once Germany's biggest submarine construction yard. Finding the bunker is not difficult and, with a large modern building on the roof, it will probably not change a great deal in the immediate future. A word of caution though: unlike many of the other structures, Hornisse does not protrude above its surroundings, a dark grey eyesore.

Instead, it is well hidden behind a number of more modern warehouses, making it possible to drive past without noticing it.

By the end of 1942, it was realised that the huge concrete monstrosities tended to attract bombers and this, together with a shortage of space, were the decisive factors for building the second Weser bunker well away from town. It was argued that there was no need for an existing railway connection and anywhere with access to the sea would do. After all, a considerable network of rails had to be laid for the construction process and there was no reason why some of this should not be left in place for bringing supplies into the bunker. With a total area of almost 50,000 square metres, Valentin became the biggest bunker in Germany, second only to the one in Brest. Building it towards the end of the war presented numerous problems and it quickly became apparent that there was a drastic shortage of everything throughout Germany. In view of this, planners had to rethink the building process to find ways of economising with materials. The concrete roof beams, for example, were almost 30 metres long, 4.5 metres high and weighed about 47 tons, making them the biggest in any of the bunkers. Doing away with as many vertical roof supports as possible was necessary to accommodate the massive assembly line for the new Type XXI, but the overriding decision in much of the design was the need to economise with materials. Consequently, Valentin used only 20 per cent of the steel that would have been consumed in comparable earlier structures in France. Despite the shortages, there appears to have been no compromise in the basic requirements as far as bomb resistance went and the concrete was made even thicker to withstand the newer bombs then being used by the Allied air forces. The shortages also stretched as far as the labour force and, in view of this, Valentin became the only bunker to be built with conscripted labour, including low-grade convicts.

Progress was considerably slower than the earlier bunker projects, but on the whole workers did achieve quite astonishing levels of efficiency. The reason for the slower building rate was that everything connected with the construction was constantly harassed by Allied aircraft, who by now were flying freely over much of Germany to attack anything in their path. It became obvious that supply wagons were much sought-after targets. Workers on building sites were also shot up and bombed as well. As a result, the workforce at Valentin is reputed to have suffered considerably, but this was not due to Germans deliberately ill-treating people. Instead, desperate shortages came about as a result of having much of the supply system destroyed or disrupted by the intensive bombing campaign. It must be borne in mind that this was taking place at a time when one single Allied air raid was killing as many people as died in Britain during the entire war. Many more were injured, made homeless or had their work places destroyed. Consequently, many innocent people suffered terrible ordeals because there was no longer any infrastructure for the usual community services.

Unlike foreign bunkers, Valentin was built to accommodate a complete assembly line for Type XXI, the large electro-boat which was due to have replaced the Types VII and IX in the Atlantic. Actually, the decision to build the bunker was made before these plans were formulated, but having done the groundwork it was resolved that at least one entire production line should be placed under concrete and the design of the building was modified for that purpose. The eight sections and other parts for making up a Type XXI, were built further inland and brought by barges, special pontoons and rail to the waterside assembly area. Since boats did not have to pass in and out, there was no need for masses of entrances along one side, and Valentin was built with as few openings as possible. Large armoured gates on the landward side provided access for the railway, and similar doors along the river allowed barges to be unloaded, while a massive dry dock facility at the end served as exit for finished boats. This was supposed to have been shut off by a stable-door type of arrangement with an armoured water gate and another one above it in case of near-misses. All this was built a distance of a few metres from the edge of the river Weser. The land on the water side was expected to have been washed away once the project was completed, but this never happened. The structure was not fully completed when the war ended.

The Royal Air Force watched the building progress with great eagerness. A number of people in Britain were hoping that the war would last long enough for them to try out the new Grand Slams. Yet, Britain must have known through Enigma decrypts that it was going to be some time before the production line would be up and running. In the end, the bomber fanatics need not have worried about losing their concrete targets. When the war ended, people living around the bunker were evacuated from their homes so that the area could become a testing ground for new bombs. The bunker had received a number of hits during the war, but most of the damage was done afterwards. However, despite aiming at an undefended target, these new massive bombs did relatively little damage and later an intensive debate focussed on the future of the site. One suggestion was that the area should be used as a dump for the rubble from the ruins in Bremen. The idea was to cover the bunker with the objective of landscaping it into a natural-looking hill. But, being a considerable distance from the town, meant this added considerably to the costs. The bunker remained a no-go area for some time, but part of it was eventually taken over by the Federal German armed forces as a warehouse. The north-easterly end, with relatively little damage, is still being used by the armed forces today – while the part with the majority of holes in the roof is left empty, the reason being that the capping of the holes would be too expensive.

Although all of the bunker is fenced off and the grounds are patrolled by armed guards with tracker dogs, it is possible to get a good view of the exterior from the perimeter fence. At the river end it is possible to walk right up to the huge opening, which was due to have been the dry dock from which completed boats would have left, and get an excellent view of the cavernous interior. With large black birds crowing in the shadows it is a most impressive sight, of incredible proportions.

HELIGOLAND (NORDSEE III)

The one and half square kilometre island of red sandstone cliffs in the North Sea has had a chequered history out of all proportion to its size. Being strategically placed in the estuaries of the Weser, Elbe, Ems and Eider, some 50 kilometres from the Friesian coast,

Heligoland had a great significance during the First World War when it was a major base for the defence of the German Bight. The island had been under British jurisdiction since 1814, when it was taken from Denmark as a result of a prolonged naval engagement, which included Admiral Nelson's famous battle of Copenhagen. In 1890, Heligoland was exchanged for Zanzibar, on the coast of East Africa, and became German. Militarisation under the Kaiser was quickly put in hand and Heligoland was turned into an impregnable naval stronghold. Although in a somewhat vulnerable position, it was a great haven for small ships, submarines and fishing boats whose still primitive and temperamental engines often required port facilities. Bearing in mind that the first endurance run of a diesel-powered U-boat from Kiel to Wilhelmshaven had taken place only a few years before the beginning of the First World War, this was a convenient harbour for any small vessel in trouble and it served as a calm anchorage for avoiding the ravages of North Sea storms. These powerful installations featured so strongly in the Treaty of Versailles that they had to be removed after the end of the war.

In 1935, when Hitler repudiated the Treaty and announced his re-armament programme, Heligoland saw a massive amount of rebuilding, with new, heavily armed strongholds being dug deep into the soft sandstone cliffs. Much of this was carried out more as a defiance of Versailles, rather than as a pressing need for defence. By that time, Heligoland had lost much of its strategic importance. New, faster aircraft, large guns and

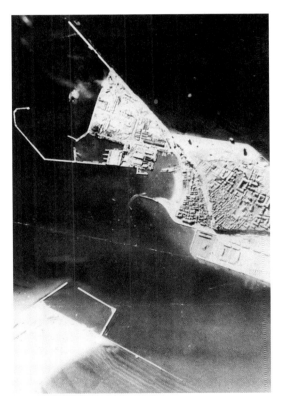

The harbour area of the island of Heligoland with the unfinished pens of the U-boat bunker visible by the side of the long curved breakwater.

The massive dimensions of the U-boat bunkers are best appreciated by standing close to them and peering up at the overpoweringly thick concrete beams. This shows the water side of the bunker at St Nazaire with an anti-aircraft battery protruding above the wall in the far distance.

other technology made it possible to bypass this exposed island. Yet, despite the drawbacks of relying on a precarious supply route running through the shallows of the Wadden sea, a U-boat bunker was built there within weeks of the outbreak of the Second World War. It never became a great strategic centre, but was often used by boats running in and out of the German estuaries. A number, for example, were damaged by ice and called in at Heligoland for divers to check propellers and rudders. However, on discovering the cause of what often was an irritating noise, boats had to travel back to Wilhelmshaven, Hamburg or Kiel for repairs. Heligoland hardly kept sufficient stocks of spare parts for operational boats.

Since the British made very little effort to interrupt this, they probably knew of the minor role which these pens were playing. Yet, the attraction of devoting a lot of resources and risking many lives for their destruction did not pass and a few weeks before the end of the war the Royal Air Force was sent in with heavy bombs to destroy the base. Most of the installations were wrecked, but people in the deep bunkers survived to be forced off the island after the war. The U-boat bunker sustained no direct hits and suffered no significant damage, but once the war was over Britain devoted considerable energy to testing its new weapons there. It would appear that people were interested in finding ways of hitting at underground installations in the sandstone, rather than striking a decisive blow against concrete. Virtually everything on the island was wrecked by being pounded into featureless pulp and, on top of that, in April 1947, two years after the end of the war, the U-boat bunker and other wartime installations were destroyed by careful demolition.

In 1952, when the wrecked remains of the island were handed back to Germany, much of the harbour had to be cleared under extremely dangerous conditions. Divers went down to break up many of these huge underwater obstacles. Not only was the space required for a new harbour, but a great deal of sharp metal was protruding, making it an unacceptable hazard for shipping. This clearing up work was accomplished so successfully that nothing remains of the U-boat bunker and no trace of it can be found today.

BREST

It is possible to get some impression of the ferocious coast around Brest by considering that the more than 600 lighthouses and navigation lights in the small area make up almost 20 per cent of the total in all of France. This scenic part of the Brittany coast is well known for sudden fogs, frequent storms, perilous rocks, treacherous currents, and consequently the marine world there is faced with well-above-average insurance premiums. None of these hazards prevented the Romans from settling there, while the countryside is littered with such a rich abundance of prehistoric remains that they must have met a good number of seafaring Gauls already firmly entrenched in the rolling countryside. The estuary of the Penfeld river in the heart of Brest makes an ideal harbour. It is a good distance from the harshness of the turbulent Atlantic and can be reached by sailing through a five kilometre-long and about two kilometre-wide channel.

The Brest bunker with heavy steel nets in the foreground. Facing a large expanse of sea meant that the bunker was most vulnerable to attacks from torpedo carrying aircraft, but these never made any effort to strike at the U-boats in the harbour.

Although this has plenty of deep water for large warships, there are a number of unexpected shallows and some rather solid rocks where one least expects them. Adding a little foul weather and a miscalculation of the tide to this combination can make the short trip into a navigator's nightmare. However, stunning rocky cliffs add to the fascination of the experience for passengers.

The narrow approach opens out into a massive, deep-water basin, some 10 kilometres wide and long enough to provide a firm anchorage for all the European fleets of the Second World War. In olden days, the narrow channel leading to this inland sea was guarded by a multitude of fortifications and it is interesting to note that both the British and Spanish fought hard to gain control of the shores. The English king, Edward III, maintained a garrison there for over half of the fourteenth century, and, two hundred years later, the famous explorer, Sir Martin Frobisher, arrived with the British fleet and an army of 4,000 to re-gain control of the anchorage. Brest not only saw a fair amount of conflict, but it was also the centre of some noteworthy innovation. The first dry dock, for example, was built there as early as 1687. Quite an achievement, especially when one considers that the majority of ships of the time were maintained below the waterline by beaching them at high tide on convenient solid ground and then waiting for the water to recede. Trying this trick in the Penfeld river is not terribly rewarding, since the tide there is nowhere near as extreme as further out, where the Atlantic waves crash against the rocks.

Sadly, it was not the town of Brest but its hinterland which prevented any large scale development of a major trading centre. The countryside failed to provide the many commodities required by a thriving city, and the absence of cross-country communications to the more populated parts of France made things more difficult. As at Kiel in north Germany, it was the navy which turned the town into a major arsenal. At first glance, the Penfeld river, with its hub of military activity, looks too insignificant for the massive fortifications which protect its mouth, but this convenient waterway twists inland for almost three kilometres, providing ample sheltered space for early seafarers. The activity there burst out of the confinement of the steep-sided valley during the

A close-up of the narrow single, dry pens at Brest, with water being pumped out of those towards the right. The drainage gear for these was one of the early weak points, being rather slow at emptying the huge basins. This problem was later overcome by fitting a channelling system so that a number of pumps could be connected to any combination of pens.

The Brest pens with the additional layer of reinforcement clearly visible on top of the original roof. The topless pyramid in the centre was part of the wartime anti-aircraft defences.

middle of the nineteenth century, when steps were taken to develop both a military and commercial port on the shores of that large inland sea. Salt water, lapping directly onto thirty metre-high cliffs, made this quite a challenge and a considerable land-reclamation project went ahead to provide the space for the necessary dockside infrastructure. This was done simply by dumping rocks at the base of the cliffs until a large enough flat surface could be created. At the same time, the area was enclosed by a couple of massive breakwaters with narrow entrances. The power of the industrial backup in that harbour can be gauged by the fact that some 32 ships were launched there during the four war years from 1914 to 1918. Following the First World War, a massive refurbishment and modernisation programme was instigated. Installing electric lighting, adding modern cranes and providing other up-to-date equipment was completed in 1939, just one year before the German navy arrived to turn it into a major U-boat base.

The Germans considered Brest to be an ideal location for U-boats and for the surface fleet, but naval planners found the long access from the landward side, over steep sided countryside, somewhat tricky. Even today, the entire dockyard area is still hemmed in by cliffs, making it difficult to reach. This became a decisive factor in the construction of submarine pens and very nearly resulted in the planners looking for an alternative port. At the time there was no easy, direct rail access, hardly enough room to manoeuvre heavy machinery and very little space to store building materials. The problem was eventually overcome by importing the majority of goods by water, pre-fabricated parts from Germany were brought to the commercial docks, five kilometres away, and carried over by barges. This took place at a time when the battleships/battlecruisers *Gneisenau*

The dry docks in Brest photographed in the year 2000 with the long mole, enclosing the military harbour, in the far distance.

and *Scharnhorst* as well as the heavy cruiser *Prinz Eugen* were in port. They attracted a good number of British bombers, which demolished quite a few of the lighters used for the building of the submarine pens.

Planners did not have a great deal of choice as far as location for the pens was concerned and quickly decided on the old seaplane station on the western extremity of the harbour. Seaplanes had their heyday long before the war, when landing in remote areas was solved by making use of the only naturally flat surfaces around. However, the unpredictability of water made the majority of operators favour land-based runways. Although the British, German and French navies devoted considerable resources to the development of floating aircraft, the problems of coping with waves continued to be troublesome and this type of transport was usually limited to smaller, reconnaissance types of planes, rather than developing fleets of long-distance amphibious bombers. Removing the seaplane base did not appear to be a great loss to either the German occupying forces nor the French, who used the base again immediately after the Kriegsmarine vacated it in 1944. The reason for wanting the bunker within the confines of the naval base was that there was already a hub of essential services. Underground fuel tanks, for example, were less than half a kilometre away. The hill behind the bunker had been hollowed out with a number of deep tunnels which provided an attractive back-up for the Germans. On top of this, the long mole sheltering the harbour from south-westerly winds also acted as a useful defence against torpedo-carrying aircraft.

Originally designed with two bays, similar to Elbe II in Hamburg, the Brest bunker was due to have been built in water and wet ground at the base of the cliffs, below the naval school. Being tidal meant the designers had to consider the same problems of allowing sufficient depth at low tide and enough headroom at high water. The double pen accommodation was quickly enlarged and the modified design was still under construction when it was altered once again. This time, the additional pens were to be made both wider and longer to accommodate larger supply submarines and the very long-range boats which were then already under construction. This was hardly underway when the plans changed once more and a special base for long-range boats was planned for Bordeaux. Enlarging the pens sounds quite straightforward, but presented the planners with considerable problems because they had started the building as far away from the centre of town as possible. This meant that it was necessary to extend sideways over a very narrow stretch of land at the base of high cliffs, working in the direction from which supplies were coming and on top of the all-important building site with cement mixers. In addition to this, it was necessary to concoct some ingenious schemes to prevent the larger pens from blocking the road and rail thoroughfares inside the bunker by building swing bridges under the thick concrete roof.

The building work, which started in 1941, was undertaken by the construction firm Julius Berger from Berlin, while local technical know-how as well as heavy plant was supplied by Campenon Bernhard of Paris. It has been suggested that the first set of two wet and two dry pens was inaugurated with great ceremony on 13 September of that same year by U372 (Kptlt Heinz-Joachim Neumann). And U83 (Kptlt Hans Werner Kraus) carried out some docking trials a few days later. However, the U-boat

The bunkered lock in St Nazaire with a cruise ship inside the huge 'Normandie lock' seen from the roof of the U-boat pens. The Normandie lock was the target for the British commando raid on St Nazaire.

A close-up of the Brest bunker showing the only part of the unfinished bomb-catching lattice. On the left is a radar tower from the wartime anti-aircraft defences and the shed-like roofs towards the right are covers over the bomb damage caused by the special earthquake bombs designed by Barnes Wallis.

The side of the Brest bunker photographed during the early summer of 2000.

The north-west corner of the Brest bunker with west gate near the pedestrian crossing. A van is coming from the long mole which encloses the military harbour to protect it from rough seas.

Command's war diary shows U372 to have arrived in Brest on 13 August 1941 and set out for sea again on 10 September. Therefore, it is likely that some other boat participated in the commissioning of the bunker. Whatever happened, this was hardly significant. The bunker was not completed until a year later and the area continued to resemble an untidy building site for some time to come.

Long before this inauguration, it was decided that the ceilings should be strengthened, but it was thought both the walls and foundations could suffer by having the additional burden piled on top. Therefore a variety of strengthening techniques were applied to different parts of the roof. Some were covered with a layer of concrete beams. Other parts, with stronger foundations, had granite blocks laid on top while additional concrete was poured onto another section. The roof received further modification in 1943 when three anti-aircraft batteries and radar towers were added. These were supported by an accommodation bunker for the gun crews and space for storing ammunition.

For most of 1942, air raids had not been too much of a problem. The first attack by a solitary aircraft towards the end of 1940 was followed by about 75 raids with over 3,000 aircraft, but in February 1942 the Royal Air Force lost interest in Brest and there followed a period of calm, probably because most of the town had been destroyed by that time and existing bombs could inflict only little damage on the might of the U-boat bunker. A few US air force bombers put in an appearance during the beginning of 1943, but following this brief annoyance, the place was left in relative peace.

By August 1944, the D-Day landings in Normandy had taken place and the might of the United States was spreading out to cut the German naval bases off from their cross-country supply routes. At that late stage, German planners instigated further modifications to the bunker. Although it sounds absurd, at this crucial moment, when armies were poised

The west side of the Brest bunker with the entrance to the right of the three pillar-like supports running up to the high section of the roof. Bomb damage from a Tallboy striking the edge of the roof can be seen about halfway along the lower section of the roof. There is an anti-aircraft emplacement for a small calibre gun on top of the roof at the extreme right-hand corner.

to capture the ports, planners in Berlin made a concerted effort to bring about another programme to increase the thickness of the roof and a contract for such a venture was awarded to the same French firm that had originally built the foundations. At the same time, while U-boats were being evacuated, the Royal Air Force embarked upon another set of intensive bombing raids, which are discussed in the chapter about bombing. These raids used not only a variety of different bombs, but also dropped mines in the harbour approaches. Consequently, there were a good number of stringent rules about manoeuvring U-boats in the port area. Some of these were so secret that they were not passed on to high ranking members of the technical staff nor to first watch officers, and resulted in at least one U-boat, U415 under Oblt.z.S. Herbert Werner, being sunk right in front of the bunker. This happened a month after D-Day, during the early morning of 14 July 1944, and killed two of the crew, seriously injuring many more. Werner was due to have taken the boat and the First Flotilla's engineering officer on trials, but failed to wake up in time. He was on his way down from his berth in the naval school on the top of the hill when he saw the terrific detonation hurl two men into the air. Apparently, the engineering officer had instructed the first watch officer to take the boat out of the bunker. Not knowing about the necessity to remain silent to prevent acoustic mines from being activated, he started the diesel engines instead of manoeuvring with the silent electric motors.

The German garrison in Brest, together with several workers from the Todt Organisation, surrendered to American troops on 21 September 1944 and shortly afterwards the French navy moved in to supervise the clearing up of the devastation in the dock yard. Although the end of the war was not yet in sight, it was realised that the facilities there would soon be required to help remove a considerable number of mines from the harbour approaches, and provisions were made to accommodate minesweeping flotillas. The Germans had given some thought to demolishing the bunker before vacating it and they had sufficient explosives in stock to render the building useless for future occupation. But there was a hospital nearby and they refrained from blowing it up to avoid endangering the lives of the people suffering there.

Finding the bunker these days is no great problem. It is stuck out on the western extremity of the naval dockyard by a long and domineering breakwater, but actually spotting the huge monstrosity can be a bit difficult. It hardly dominates its surroundings, like the majority of the other bunkers. Instead, it is well hidden below some prominent cliffs leading up to the commanding position of the naval school. Brest is still a major naval base, and much of the military harbour is definitely off limits for casual visitors, except on well-publicised open days, when the public is welcome to inspect the facilities. However, it is possible to get exceptionally fine views of the bunker from public roads, so visiting the site does not end in disappointment. The great trick with an exploration tour by vehicle is to travel from east to west, otherwise an obstinate one-way system will frustrate the effort. Immediately after crossing the imposing lift bridge over the Penfeld river one is confronted with an entrance to the naval dock yard and a high, somewhat ugly wall, probably a remnant from Napoleonic days. Yet this obstruction does not reach far and is later replaced by a high iron fence made up of white-painted vertical bars, wide enough apart to get a good view of the spot where so much history has been made. The public road along the edge of the dockyard climbs steadily up the hill to provide excellent views of the massive stretch of water beyond the breakwater. Following this, it is not difficult to spot the dark remains of the bunker rising high above a number of more modern buildings, The road also offers an excellent opportunity to examine the full length of the bunker's back wall. What is more, it climbs up above roof level, providing an excellent opportunity of studying this in detail. There is public access to the sea at the western edge of the naval dockyard, but the long breakwater is unfortunately on the wrong side of the fence for walking along. A road runs up a valley from the western dockyard gate and the hill on the opposite side of this is of special interest because it is where the underground fuel dumps used to be located.

The town of Brest makes a most pleasant impression, with an above-average abundance of bars, at least one well-stocked naval bookshop, and friendly people. The ramparts along the edge of the hill also provide magnificent views of both the Penfeld river and the vast, open, inland sea.

LORIENT

Lorient grew up during the middle of the seventeenth century as a new town overflow for Port Louis on the mouth of Blavet river. It was said that the prominence remained at the seaside while workers, merchants and pretty girls moved inland to where there was more room for expansion. With its main hive of activity firmly focussed on the busy port

U618 nosing its way towards the bunkers in Lorient. Keroman III is clearly visible on the right, while the one and only single sea entrance of Keroman I is visible in the far distance. This was situated by the left-hand corner as one looks at the bunker from the water. The low tower on top of the roof above berth 24 of Keroman III held an anti-aircraft battery.

The landward side of Keroman I in Lorient was the only U-boat bunker on 'dry land' where boats had to be hauled out of the water in order to fit inside. This had the advantage that it was unnecessary to book dry dock times for below the waterline repairs such as this. All boats going into Keroman I were hauled out of the water, placed on a many-wheeled buggy and then transported into the bunker by a sliding bridge system. Although most vulnerable, this was never sabotaged nor seriously damaged by bombing. The boat is U123.

U306 under Kptlt Claus von Trotha in front of the Scorff bunker in Lorient. Although it looks as if the extended periscope is going to collide with the roof, the interior was high enough for these to be pulled out.

The Scorff bunker is easily identified because it is the only one with that characteristic protrusion above the central wall. This has not been added as decoration but is part of the protection for the anti-aircraft defences, housing a small-calibre gun.

with warehouses filled with delicacies from the Far East, it became known as L'Orient (The East) until some inspiring authority decided that this was also a good name and shortened it to Lorient. During the middle of the eighteenth century, Britain took such a deep interest in its development that a fleet, with an army on board, was sent there to curtail the French activities so that the competition would not interfere with home trade. Although a successful landing took place, the invasion appears to have been a half-hearted affair and the attackers withdrew at a time when the small garrison was on the verge of surrendering. Although delighted by the victory, the French did not rest on their laurels and set about strengthening the defences to make the town into a fortified arsenal. Sadly, while this was going on, trade dropped off and Lorient degenerated into what an early twentieth century report described as 'a place with only a few features of interest'. One of the decisive problems was that the growing town was backed up by a relatively sparse hinterland, which could support only subsistence agriculture and forestry. This resulted in a lucrative trade in pit props for South Wales mines, which were paid for with coal, and led to the building of a special wharf with good rail connections to handle the heavy, dirty goods, but did little to bring prosperity to the town.

Shortly before the Second World War, the majority of the 46,000 people in Lorient were employed either by the military, by the docks or in the massive fishing harbour. This was indeed a major, relatively recent innovation to inject new life into the flagging economy and paid dividends by making Lorient one of the biggest and most important fishing ports in France. Boulogne toppled it from the top of the ratings ladder, but Lorient still lands one of the most expensive catches with an exceptionally wide variety of species. It was this fishing port which caught the German's attention, when they started looking around for a U-boat base. The harbour was well suited for fishermen and U-boats because of its relatively sheltered position, some five kilometres inland from the raging Atlantic. The approach was guarded from the most frequent and blusterous south-westerlies by the Ile de Groix, a small island which also had a German signalling station for U-boats coming home with broken radios. The idea being that visual contact should be made before embarking upon the hazardous voyage inland.

Penetrating the channel was not easy, especially in the face of determined opposition. The water between Kerneve and Port Louis is only a little over half a kilometre wide, with the navigable channel restricted to less than half of that. The currents of up to four knots are no worse than many other harbour approaches, but this stretch of water challenges the best of mariners by having times when the surface water is flowing out while the tide is running in. This happens especially during wet periods when there is so much force washing down the rivers that it overpowers the incoming tide and pushes it down to the bed. Thus the surface current flowing out to sea is gradually lifted by the rising tide sweeping in below it to produce some rather unusual navigational hazards. The approach to these narrows is also well guarded by a number of well-positioned rocks, right in the middle of what locks like a deep water channel, and great care must be taken to avoid these or join the multitude of wrecks who discovered them when it was too late. Once past the narrowest point, the river opens into a large, mud-lined basin with ample room for manoeuvring. It is only as one approaches the Scorff river by the town of Lorient that shipping runs into further problems with annoying shallows. Before the war, these had become such an annoyance that constant dredging was required to keep the channel open.

After the French naval base, together with dry docks and shipbuilding facilities, grew up by the sides of the Scorff river, someone came up with a special type of double lock for building ships. The idea being that hulls could be floated out, rather than being launched, because the river was too narrow for conventional slips. The biggest dry dock in Lorient was 192 metres long, making it a rather tight fit for even a pocket battleship at 188 metres. The pocket battleships' draught of 7 metres would also have presented embarrassing problems on the shallows at low tide and a port with slightly more generous proportions was preferred for such big ships. The battleships-cum-battlecruisers *Scharnhorst* and *Gneisenau* had a length of 235 metres and heavy cruisers were 206 metres long, meaning they would not have fitted in at all.

U-boats, of course, did not have these size problems, fitting very well into the limitations of Lorient. Indeed U30, under Kptlt Fritz-Julius Lemp, arrived there on 7 June 1940, shortly after the capitulation, to become the first U-boat to be supplied in a French occupied port. The special train with spare parts, torpedoes and other supplies, which had been prepared for the purpose left Wilhelmshaven to arrive shortly before Lemp.

A close up of the single water entrance of Keroman I. This huge gateway was situated on the left hand side of the bunker as one looks at it from the sea and the main body of the building stretched away towards the right. In the foreground are the floats of a torpedo net.

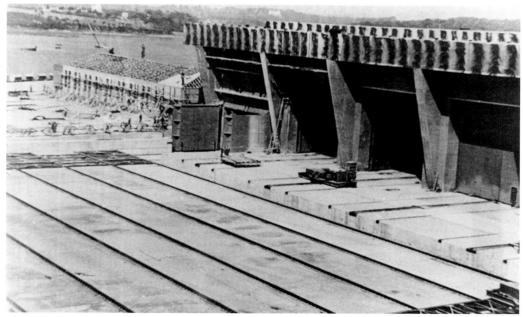

Looking down from the roof of Keroman I on to the eight-rail system for moving buggies with U-boats, and the landlocked Keroman II bunker on the right. The set of low doors at the far left were for storing and repairing the many-wheeled buggies for carrying the U-boats, while the higher doors were tall enough to accommodate a large ocean-going submarine of Type IXC.

A position on the west side of the Scorff river was chosen for one of the U-boat bunkers. Named after the river, its operational life was somewhat turbulent and turned into a can of worms for the Kriegsmarine. Being in a hurry to get the job done, the Todt Organisation turned to German firms for the construction and thus got themselves entangled with the first problems. It appears that the management of the consortium was not as hot as the planners from the Todt organisation were led to believe and much of the machinery stood around idle for weeks on end. Consequently the programme quickly started running behind schedule. Dr Todt wasn't impressed by what he saw when he inspected the site and wrote a terse letter to get things moving.

The idea was to ram almost 3,000 steel beams into relatively solid ground, some 10 metres from tidal river's edge, build the bunker on top and then dredge away the earth to allow access to the water. At the same time the interior of the bunker was dug out. Speed of construction was the main reason for choosing this method, which would have been quite good, had the Germans not chosen a site where silt collected quickly in great quantities. Both the area in front of the bunker and the interior had to be dredged frequently to keep the access clear and to prevent U-boats from grounding at low tide. The other problem came to light once the building was well under way and it was realised the ceilings were nowhere near thick enough for modern bombs. The quick method of sinking the foundations did not allow for a great deal of extra weight and it was thought that the structure could not bear a reinforced ceiling. Therefore it was a case of hoping that bombs would miss or that the Allies would not be interested in the relatively small building.

Today, the double-pen Scorff bunker still lies within the naval dockyard, making access for tourists a problem. A low bridge by its side can be used by locals as a shortcut

The entrance to Keroman III at Lorient, seen from U618.

The inside of Keroman III, showing one of the pens with direct access to the water.

Interior 'dockside' equipment at Keroman III.

from town centre to the western suburbs, but the guards are not allowed to permit foreign cars across. Therefore, it was suggested that we should park outside the dockyard and walk through, but that was frustrated by the presence of a camera, which made it obvious that we were not locals hurrying over to the other side. However, the guard was very nice and apologised for having to turn us away, saying that although we are all Europeans now, there are small parts of France where a French passport is still necessary. Being barred from the road through the dockyard was not too much of a disappointment, since one can get a reasonable view of the bunker from the banks of the river, a short distance to the north.

The fishing harbour at Keroman, a couple of kilometres downstream from the Scorff bunker, was completed during the late 1920s and presented the German navy with brilliant opportunities for creating a first class U-boat base. Not only were rail connections in place, but much of the area had been landscaped with modern facilities and plenty of open spaces for additional buildings. The whole project involved a fair amount of land reclamation, the building of new quays, and it also left a large undeveloped patch on top of a natural granite-cored promontory, making the terrain ideal for building a heavy bunker without having to spend too much time sinking deep foundations.

The fishing harbour had a rather fascinating innovation. There was a ramp for pulling boats of up to 65 metres long out of the water. They were floated onto a submerged, many-wheeled buggy, looking somewhat like a well-shod, overweight millipede. This, together with the boat in piggyback position, was then pulled onto a massive turntable so

The U-boat Command headquarters at Kernevel near Lorient. Although originally a requisitioned house, the place was strengthened with a massive bunker to accommodate the vital nerve centre of the U-boat Arm.

A close-up of the massive turntable at the centre of the Dombunker *complex.*

The eight-rail wagon for sliding buggies with U-boats in and out of the two bunkers, Keroman I towards the left and Keroman II on the right. The low armoured doors of the buggy bay are still visible in the far distance on the right. The other armoured doors have been replaced by glass partitions to let in light so that the bunker can be used for commercial purposes.

that it could be rotated and lined up with one of several repair bays. Type II U-boats were 44 metres long and Type VII 66.5 metres, but these bigger boats had a considerable 'overhang' at the back, over the rudders and propellers, making this an ideal substitute for the general shortage of dry docks. Submarines lying on land could attract bombers and their comparatively bulky profile made them large targets for flying splinters. This potential disaster was solved by covering two of the repair bays with concrete, making them look like windowless churches. Being short of a name, the Germans called them just that, but their size suggested they should be something a bit more superior than a mere church. Whence they were called Dombunker, meaning cathedral or dome bunker. With walls of no less than 1.5 metres thick towards the top, and even more massive at the base, meant that they were strong enough to resist near-misses. The roof curved in such a manner that it was highly unlikely that a bomb would explode directly on it because it was more likely to bounce off first.

Whilst the Dombunkers have an almost passive appearance, if one ignores their thickly armoured doors, the rest of the Keroman complex dominates the surroundings considerably and gives the impression of intimidating anyone who dares approach too close. The basic set-up of this overpowering base differs a great deal from the other bunkers, making it somewhat confusing to understand. It is important to bear in mind that there are three separate, detached bunkers, named Keroman I, II and III, and two more were in the planning stage but never finished.

Keroman I has one single entrance on the seaward edge and six pens on the opposite or landward side. Keroman II was built about a hundred metres inland from Keroman I

The many-wheeled buggy bay with armoured doors still in situ, photographed during the early summer of 2000. This part of the bunker was being used as a commercial warehouse.

and the space between the two is still occupied by an eight-tracked railway system with a large bridge that could be moved sideways. Having entered the single entrance in Keroman I, submarines were floated on top of a many-wheeled cradle, to be hauled out of water, up a 1:10 incline. The cradle, with U-boat on top, was then pulled on to this eight-tracked railway system to be shunted sideways until it lined up with one of the accommodation boxes in Keroman I or II. Once in position, the submarine was hauled under cover of the bunker. The whole process took less than 90 minutes and the time spent on the exposed rail system in the middle was usually much less than an hour, but still it is difficult to see why the planners came up with this vulnerable combination. A serious bomb hit in this critical area could easily have isolated boats in all the pens and prevented them from being carried back into the water. Luckily, the problem never arose and the system worked well, other than that it was impossible for the larger boats to get in or out at extreme low tide because the water at the entrance was too shallow. The roof was too low in the majority of pens for pulling out periscopes and a special facility with high-level crane was provided in part of the bunker. Keroman III was a conventional bunker with five dry and two wet pens, holding a maximum of 12 U-boats.

Hauling boats out of the water and keeping them on dry land had several advantages. The first, and most important, was that it saved a considerable amount of time. To dry dock a boat in a conventional system, where water had to be pumped out of a large concrete box, took up to five hours and filling it again took almost as long. On the other hand, a boat could be hauled out of the water much quicker. This was most useful for those many rapid inspections which were necessary to check underwater parts when the interior of a U-Boat had sustained considerable depth charge damage, but where there were no obvious signs of external complications.

As with many of the other bunkers, building started before the requirements for the basic design were thought out and modifications, as well as additions, were considered as the construction got under way. Consequently, the clean, sweeping sides of the building were quickly cluttered up with a number of extensions. Power came from the civilian grid in the form of high voltage and a number of necessary transformers had to be accommodated in the bunker. In addition to this, a steam turbine driving a generator and a number of diesel engines for emergency power supplies were installed as well as a central heating plant. Fuel, water and a variety of oil tanks, a plant for making distilled water for topping up batteries and a number of offices were added. It was also planned to place a Fangrost or set of concrete bomb catching beams on the roof, but this modification never got underway. The building process went relatively smoothly, although a considerable unforeseen effort had to be made with the entrance for Keroman I, which required extensive and highly specialized blasting to remove large lumps of granite. While this was going on, a narrow-gauge railway helped in removing the overburden for sinking the foundations and this ran into the first major snags. There was not as much granite as the initial survey had led to believe and parts of the complex were without this rather solid foundation. Therefore pile-drivers had to be brought in to sink a number of 20 metre-long beams into the ground. Many of the metal parts, especially the beams for the roof, were made in Germany and assembled close to the building site. All this ran so smoothly that

The Eastern Dombunker *and massive turntable with one of the many-wheeled buggies for carrying ships onto dry land.*

The Eastern Dombunker *has been converted into a four-floored warehouse by breaking up the end and removing the heavy armoured doors.*

the first trials with the ramp in Keroman I, for hauling large Type IX boats out of the water, were carried out on 25 August 1941 with U123 under Kptlt Reinhard Hardegen. The inauguration of the bunker followed ceremoniously on 1 September.

The Royal Air Force had known about the goings-on in Lorient and had been making an effort to plaster critical areas with bombs since September 1940, some six months after the Kriegsmarine first arrived. There were even a few direct hits on the bunkers, but most of the damage was to the surrounding areas and town, where the supporting infrastructure was disrupted. In the end, the ravages of time caused the biggest headache for bunker maintenance, but the Germans had departed by then and it was the French government which footed the bill for covering large parts with metal netting. The reason being that both walls and roofs started flaking so badly that large pieces are now continuously falling down and could lead to the death or serious injury of unsuspecting passers-by. The Keroman bunkers remained fenced off and out of bounds until the end of the twentieth century when the French ministry of defence shrunk its services and started withdrawing from the site. Parts are now used as commercial warehouses and an interesting stern trawler museum has started to invade. In addition to this, conducted tours around the site, including walks through the interior, are being organised. Although Keroman I, II and III remain fenced off, the guards did not stop anyone wandering in through a ghost town relic of a naval base. Half a dozen well-armed policemen showed no interest in a number of casual visitors exploring the fascinating remains of the Battle of the Atlantic. Peering out at the vast expanse of water, it is hard to believe that the ocean lies several kilometres away and the vast open space in front of the bunkers is nothing more than a river estuary with an abundance of seaweed and all the usual paraphernalia one associates with salt water. A new road has been built down to the fishing harbour and finding the bunkers is easy, since they dominate the surroundings by towering high above the other industrial buildings.

ST NAZAIRE

In 1856 St Nazaire erupted out of an isolated and insignificant small fishing village to become a major port with one of the biggest floating harbours in Europe. At that time, the land on which Wilhelmshaven has been built had only recently been purchased by Prussia from the Grand Duchy of Oldenburg and the plans for the development of the naval base were still on the drawing board. The German nation had not yet been founded and still consisted of a number of independent kingdoms and principalities. Yet, the Brandtaucher, Prussia's first submarine built by the Bavarian artillery officer, Wilhelm Bauer, had already been lying on the seabed at Kiel for almost six years, having been launched and sunk in 1850.

The main reason for the explosion of progress at St Nazaire was the temperamental river Loire, whose sandbanks had started preventing larger ships from making the fifty kilometre long passage inland to the seaport of Nantes. Later, once steam-powered dredgers were invented, a drastic effort was made to reinstate this major port as a centre

A boat nudging its way into berth 12B at St Nazaire. The success pennants fluttering from the periscope suggest that it is on its way in, rather than at the beginning of a new voyage.

of commerce, but by that time it was too late. The new harbour at St Nazaire had captured the majority of the traffic. This was not as impressive as many people had anticipated and, despite a considerable injection of money, remained a very much one-sided business, relying more or less exclusively on imports. Although there were good berthing facilities with two and half kilometres of non-tidal and two kilometres of tidal quays, all with an adequate supply of cranes, there were no specialised loading facilities nor the type of warehousing expected from such a grand commercial centre.

St Nazaire was still in its development stages when the economic impact of the Industrial Revolution arrived, in the shape of growing competition from other ports around the globe. The development of the harbour was begun at a time when wooden walls with sails still dominated the seas, but the next fifty years saw the coming of steam, iron ships and consequently the launching of new floating monstrosities. During the First World War, St Nazaire became a major port for the disembarkation of Canadian and American troops, probably because some notable passenger terminals had been built to attract the increasingly lucrative ocean liner trade. Yet all this was to no avail. Progress was faster than the development of St Nazaire and new ocean giants could not cross the shallows in the Loire estuary, nor fit through the locks leading into the floating harbour.

A desperate attempt was made by the French building firm Chantiers de St Nazaire Penhoët to rectify this problem in order to compete with the growing world market and,

The rear of the bunker at St Nazaire showing the multitude of railway lines used for bringing in building materials for the bunker and supplies for U-boats.

The Hotel Royal in La Baule where the 7th U-Flotilla established their radio and communications room, first under the leadership of Lt.z.S. Martin Scholtz and later under Lt.z.S. Erhard Konrad.

during the late 1920s, they started building a massive lock to connect the larger, inner basin of the harbour with the sea. This had the double function of also serving as a construction lock for the biggest of passenger liners. The three-funnelled *Normandie* was built there during the early 1930s and then the lock was used to assemble the 35,000 ton battleship, *Jean Bart*. These monumental undertakings made it necessary also to deepen the channel leading out to sea by several metres, but this injection of new life into an inadequate port was neutralised by the outbreak of the Second World War.

This huge lock was the only dry dock on the entire west coast of France large enough to hold the German battleships *Bismarck* and *Tirpitz*, and consequently became a considerable thorn in the flesh for Britain. German raiders and even poorly armed auxiliary cruisers had been reaping havoc in the British shipping lanes and the possibility of such massive battleships at large was intimidating. It was known that *Bismarck* was on her way to St Nazaire to seek out the services of the dry dock, and enormous resources were employed to sink her. Not knowing whether such action would succeed a second time, Britain decided to pre-empt any plans for bringing *Tirpitz* into the Atlantic, by barring her from the only dry dock on the Atlantic coast. But the giant lock seemed to be an impossible nut to crack. It was built with reinforced concrete on top of hard natural rock, with welded, sideways sliding gates. Whatever the Royal Air Force could throw at this would hardly scratch the surface. The large earthquake bombs, designed by Barnes Wallis, had not yet made an appearance on the official drawing board, suggesting that the

U552, the Red Devil Boat, commanded first by Kptlt. Erich Topp, then by Kptlt Klaus Popp and later by Oblt.z.S. Günther Lube in front of the bunker at St Nazaire.

destruction of the lock would be an apparently impossible undertaking. However, the threat of *Tirpitz* in the Atlantic was so intimidating that Britain overcame the problem by dispatching a combined operations demolition team, together with an old destroyer, HMS *Campbeltown*, packed full of explosives, to be rammed into the lock. This took place on 27 March 1942, about a month after the famous Channel Dash, when the battleships-cum-battlecruisers *Gneisenau* and *Scharnhorst*, together with the heavy cruiser *Prinz Eugen* made their daring homeward run from Brest.

Building a U-boat bunker in the original, southern basin of the floating harbour at St Nazaire was only partly a good idea, but the disadvantages were not as great as they seemed at first sight. The main reason being that the harbour was built on top of an old arm of the Loire and its bed was as deep as the surrounding river. Therefore, should the locks be smashed, there would still be tidal access to the bunker. In many ways it seems strange that not more effort was made to damage the locks, but throughout the war there appears to have been very little interference with these vulnerable parts of the delicate chain. Only the south lock was damaged on one occasion and temporarily put out of action during March 1943. The Germans went to considerable lengths to overcome this weakness of vulnerable locks by adding new bunkered locks to all their floating U-boat harbours. However, these bunkered locks were not completed until early to mid-1944, so they made virtually no contribution to the overall war effort. Building them was also a

Looking from the top of the main bunker towards the bunkered lock and the smaller eastern lock. Although now obsolete, the bunkered lock is used as a museum and houses a most attractive treasure in the form of a French post war submarine. The Normandie Lock, which was the main target for the famous raid on St Nazaire, lies just behind and towards the left, and is still in use to this day, as a repair base for large ocean-going ships. The round, knob-like protrusion almost in the middle of the back of the bunker is an armoured steel turret.

The bunker at St Nazaire seen from the side of the large southern lock. Although an incredibly impressive example of massive architecture, the bunker is dwarfed by the modern industrial plant behind it.

The bomb-catching grid was made up of a large number of supporting walls, seen here running from left to right, with the bomb-catching beams on top. Both the dimensions of the beams as well as the height of supporting walls varies from being relatively small towards the right of this picture to quite massive structures further towards the centre of the roof. The idea of this bomb-catching grid was to prevent bombs from bouncing off and damaging vulnerable services such as railway lines.

comparatively long-winded affair, with the excavations having started as early as October 1942. This is indeed a considerable time when one considers that the first four pens of the main shelter in St Nazaire were built in four months, to make them the first bunkers outside Germany to be used operationally (on 30 June 1941). On that day, Dr Fritz Todt and Vizeadmiral Karl Dönitz, the U-boat Chief, watched U203 under Kptlt Rolf Mützelburg slide under the concrete, accompanied by the roaring music of a military band and the loud cheers from a large watching crowd. Construction had stopped, the workers had been given a holiday, and a party with an ample supply of beer was laid on.

The building site had been cordoned off from the water in the port basin by driving two curved lines of steel shuttering into the bed. The tops of both sides were then secured to one another and filled with sand to look like a series of cylinders standing upright in the water. This enabled excavations to go ahead in record time and for both dry and wet pens to be constructed. A number of both small and large pumps were provided for emptying and filling those berths fitted with lock gates. The pipework allowed the pumps to be connected to different docks or for all of them to pump just one, filling or emptying one dock in less than 90 minutes. In addition to this there was the usual set of emergency electricity generators powered by diesel engines. The main transformer bringing in power from the town's supply was almost a kilometre to the north of the main bunker. As with the other bases, the bunker started as a plain box for accommodating U-boats and then had a number of extensions added. The most notable being areas where heavy shipyard repair work could be undertaken. The roof was strengthened considerably in June 1943, first by adding another few metres of concrete and then by placing a bomb-catching grid over the top, but less than half of this was completed by the time the war along the Biscay coast came to an end.

One wonders whether it was owing to the natural instinct of humans to bolt the stable door after the horse had gone, that the bunkered lock at St Nazaire was given such unusually heavy fortifications, with the facility of being able to train a number of quite large guns out into the approaches. In addition to the usual gun slits, there was an armoured dome on the roof and four anti-aircraft towers. This was quite considerable, especially when one considers that there were only two anti-aircraft emplacements on top of the main bunker, from where gunners had a better view of approaching aircraft. The bunkered lock was also built by the same method of building what looked like cylinders filled with sand around the site to keep the water at bay. However, here the tops of those cylinders were covered with a thick layer of concrete, just in case a bomb exploded in a critical spot to disrupt the proceedings by scattering the sand and thus allowing water to flood into the building site.

When the war ended, St Nazaire had to nurse numerous wounds from incessant air raids which had destroyed much of the town. The bunker was put to a number of uses, first serving as an emergency warehouse and later as accommodation for small boats. By the year 2000, considerable thought had gone into this major eyesore and steps were taken to convert it into an attractive feature of the modern town. This was an immense undertaking, since it was not easy to hide such a massive structure. First, the back walls

Looking across from the bunkered lock towards the U-boat pens in St Nazaire, with the smaller, eastern lock in the foreground. The large, southern lock is a few hundred metres towards the left. This bunker has those rather narrow, closed-in workshop areas between some of the pens, which can be seen here towards the left.

from a number of pens were removed to allow easy access from the landward side. This involved considerable noise with pneumatic drills hammering away for weeks on end. Large saws, for cutting through stubborn concrete reinforced with large granite chips, were employed to cut through other parts. Incidentally this cement mix has stood up better against the ravages of time than the concoction used in Lorient. There appears to be less flaking, with only very little need to cover the walls with netting to prevent pieces falling down. Some small nets for catching flaking concrete can be seen, but they are certainly nowhere near as dominant as in Lorient.

A large ramp has been built, to bring people and even fair-sized vehicles on to the roof, where fencing has been erected for a walkway. This is rather magnificent, offering ample opportunities to explore the bomb-catching grid, and the roof provides excellent views of the harbour. In fact, it is an ideal location for reading the *After the Battle* edition on the St Nazaire Raid.[1] Virtually everything mentioned in its description can be seen from the roof of the bunker. The interesting point about this edition of *After the Battle* and the issue on U-boat bases is that they were compiled in 1988 and 1987 respectively, and are now history themselves. The 'modern' pictures in these issues are still recognisable, but so much has changed that they provide a fascinating glimpse into the path of progress.

[1] See Bibliography, page 193.

The inside of a pen in the St Nazaire bunker with seriously flaking walls during the spring of 2000. A major problem with large chunks of concrete falling off, some parts of the bunkers have been covered with stout wire netting.

The bunkered lock now houses a submarine museum. The French S-637 *Espadon* was moved to St Nazaire after its decommissioning to serve as a museum exhibit, and is well worth a visit. She was launched in 1958, a modification of the German Type XXI, and makes a fascinating comparison with a similar boat in Folkestone, but of Russian nationality. In addition to this there are similar British boats in Chatham and at Birkenhead, making this an interesting addition to the group. Oddly, however, there is very little reference to the turbulent past under German rule. So little of the wartime buildings remains that is now exceedingly difficult to work out where some of the old photographs were taken. Not only has St Nazaire been rebuilt, but the old and somewhat antiquated road pattern has been changed to meet modern demands. Despite this, there is no shortage of concrete bunkers, old railway tracks half embedded in new road surfaces and the odd trace of a building which survived the bombing offensive to make a tour of St Nazaire most interesting.

LA PALLICE

Ex-U-boat men still talk about the bunker at La Rochelle, although it was actually at La Pallice, some six kilometres to the west of the old port. This confusion was probably as a result of the bunker being surrounded by nothing more than a smattering of nondescript warehouses in an otherwise splendid industrial isolation. The facilities of town,

The dock basin at La Pallice seen from the gates of the one and only lock leading into this rectangular floating harbour. Being so vulnerable to air attack, the Germans built another bunkered lock by the side of the original entrance. The original, left-hand part of the bunker was operational but the right-hand extension had not yet been completed.

U275 under Oblt.z.S. Helmut Bork nearest the bunker at La Pallice.

accommodation, entertainment and the pretty girls were based firmly in the comfortable and ancient town centre, and La Rochelle is a fairytale town one is unlikely to forget. Complete with medieval walls, ramparts and romantic towers, it has the perfect 'pirates' lair' type of harbour. Take away the few modern trappings and one is left with the ideal set for making any swashbuckling sailing film. The sheltered, tidal harbour at La Rochelle is guarded by two imposing medieval towers and this picturesque scene, with its dreamy quays, old houses and a mass of modern yachts, successfully hides the two floating harbours with their commercial trappings. Although still in use at the beginning of the war, this centre of trade had seen its heyday a hundred years earlier when there was still an abundance of ships which could fit through the small, antiquated locks.

Having been under both French and English jurisdiction, La Rochelle has had a chequered history. It belonged to the English crown from 1152 to 1226 and again for a decade towards the end of the following century. But there was no peace there, even when the French had it to themselves. The predominantly Protestant faith in the town did not go down too well with the Catholic monarchy and, rather than live as Christians, a Royal army besieged the town for six months in 1572 and there was another attack lasting 15 months in 1628–9. Since marauding Christians tortured followers of other churches, the people of La Rochelle did not capitulate until there was virtually no one left to man the defences. The fact that the population dropped from 27,000 to less than 5,000 would suggest that the inhabitants were either fanatically determined or

U333 in one of the dry pens at La Pallice with work being undertaken on the propellers and rear hydroplanes. U333 had five different commanders, the most famous being 'Ali' Cremer, a Knight of the Iron Cross. He had the distinction of having accidentally sunk the German blockade breaker Spreewald *and collided three times with enemy ships in the Atlantic!*

U571 under Oblt.z.S. of the Reserve Helmut Block in front of the bunker at La Pallice and the floats of the massive torpedo net in the foreground. A smaller bunker, housing an electricity transformer for the U-boat base, can be seen to the left of the tall chimney in the middle of the picture.

The bunker at La Pallice photographed from the southern side, showing the three-pen extension which was added later and resulted in the floating harbour having to be enlarged by digging away several hundred metres of soil from this side of the basin.

exceedingly foolhardy. The dying-off of so many defenders meant there were not enough workers to maintain the infrastructure of the town and it fell into a steady decline lasting the best part of a hundred years. A considerable effort was then made to revitalise the harbour. Consequently, La Rochelle rose in importance and prosperity, but sadly most of this progress was taking place against a general decline in world trade. The advantages of being a leading French port became minimal and it was virtually only the traffic to and from Canada and Louisiana which kept the port in business. Canada then came under British jurisdiction and the Pelican State was sold to the United States, making matters even worse.

The first floating harbour at La Rochelle was opened in 1808 and the second one in 1864, shortly after a railway connection had been built. Yet, the relatively small port, with access limited to high tide for most ships, meant there were no prospects of competing with the more predominant harbours further along the coast, so the Chamber of Commerce took the decision to built a new, deep water port at La Pallice. At the same time, steps were taken to construct a passenger pier with railway terminal further out in the tidal basin so that ships could call without having to put up with the time-consuming process of passing through the lock. This was and still is 235 metres long and 21.5 metres wide. However, the lock gates take up some of this space and the maximum length which could fit in is 170 metres. Once inside the floating harbour there were 37 cranes, a grain elevator and two dry docks with adequate facilities. Being the second deepest port along the west French coast meant La Pallice could take virtually any ship which was neither too wide nor too long for the lock. What was more, there were virtually no tidal limitations on approaching the harbour and the only problem arose when there was a strong south-westerly blowing over an ebbing tide. Under such conditions, the sea is likely to become somewhat choppy, making it a none-too happy experience for casual tourists. That hardly worried the hardened U-boat crews.

The construction of the U-boat bunker started in April 1941. A double row of curved metal shuttering was rammed into the middle of the floating harbour, a similar technique to that used at St Nazaire. There was very little sludge on top of solid bedrock, making it possible to dispense with the laying of foundations. Instead, a concrete raft was laid to level the site and the walls built on top. The advantage with La Pallice over St Nazaire was that there was ample open space for the construction site and most of the structures, such as roof trusses, could be assembled close by, instead of having to be imported from satellite building areas. This made for speedier progress and it was just six months later, in October 1941 when the first pens were ready for occupation. By the time U82 (Kptlt Siegfried Rollmann) arrived on 19 November to inaugurate the new facilities, the other five pens were almost ready as well.

The imposing generator hall, measuring some 30 x 50 metres and a gigantic 25 metres high, was not finished until the spring of the following year. By that time work had already started on an extension at the back of the bunker and the addition of three more pens onto the southern side. This was considerably more time-consuming than building the first part of the bunker because it involved considerable excavation work. At the time when the first part of the bunker was built it occupied the entire harbour width and the

The large, thick-walled bunker for housing an electrical transformer by the side of the U-boat pens in La Pallice.

extension made it necessary to enlarge the dock basin by digging away 250 metres of solid ground in front. While this was underway, work continued on the first part to thicken the roof and to add a bomb-catching grid. The additional concrete was poured on to the roof, but the grid was never completed.

In June 1942, work started on building a bunkered lock by the side of the existing entrance and this was finished in March 1944, just three months before the allied D-Day invasion of Normandy. Being the southernmost of the northerly Biscay ports, meant that the lock and bunker saw considerable activity towards this critical period of the war, when a number of boats escaped from Brest and Lorient to call on La Pallice before making the dangerous voyage to Norway. The reason for calling at La Pallice was that these boats brought out specialists and valuable equipment which made them too heavy and cramped for longer voyages.

Immediately after the war, the bunker was used commercially and by the French navy, but in the year 2000 it looked not only very much the worse for wear, but also somewhat deserted. Many of the pens were occupied with rusting hulks and the original German cranes were still in situ, but somewhat rusty. Pigeons, making a bid for world domination, had made the bunker their global headquarters. There seemed to be more of them than in Trafalgar Square, and the vast mass of droppings, up to 10–30 cm deep in places, suggested that the birds had been undisturbed for some time. The whole site is a mysterious and somewhat extraordinary blend of modern, old and sheer neglect. On the one hand there is an active wood depot, as well as a number of ultra-modern warehouses with well-used railway lines. Yet, there are a number of old doors with modern signs which obviously have not been opened for some time. Of the anti-submarine or anti-

Looking from the central jetty of the La Pallice bunker towards the south, showing the interior of the more recent extension.

The ceiling of the lock bunker at La Pallice. There is very little to see because the majority of the steel beams have vanished into the concrete and all that is left down below are the bottom edges of the beams and the corrugated iron shuttering which held the near-liquid concrete in place.

A somewhat unusual small bunker with impressively thick walls by the side of the railway, close to the U-Boat pens at La Pallice, now used as a shed.

The tidal, seaward side of the bunkered lock at La Pallice.

The northern side of the La Pallice bunker showing the reinforced roof, entrance to the pens and, in the foreground, a torpedo net of relative modern design. Close by was another net of the type used by the Kriegsmarine during the war.

La Pallice in 2000, with semi-sunk stern trawler lying in front of the pens. The whole bunker looked as if it had gone through a time warp with modern industry all around apparently taking no notice of this relic from Europe's turbulent past.

torpedo nets lying around, one was of modern design, but another was made according to the pattern used by the Kriegsmarine during the war. Even some of the wartime paintwork is still clearly visible on the outside. There were surprisingly few indications of vandalism and a dubious looking vagrant, roaming around, kept his distance without making the slightest effort to interfere with visitors.

La Pallice was also the setting for the film, *Das Boot* (The Boat). The final scenes of the boat sinking in front of the reception party were filmed in front of the bunkered lock.

BORDEAUX

A population of slightly over a quarter of a million and almost the same numbers living in the surrounding area made Bordeaux the fourth largest city in France when the Second World War started. Almost seventy years earlier, when France declared war on Prussia, and again in 1914, at the outbreak of the First World War, the government moved from Paris to this thriving seaport, to be out of reach of invading armies. Although the city lies almost 100km from the coast, a number of better placed locations nearer the mouth of the Gironde river have never succeeded in sucking all the trade away from this old centre. Even during the Second World War, when Vizeadmiral Karl Dönitz and representatives from the Todt Organisation reconnoitred the full length of the Gironde estuary, they still chose Bordeaux as a U-boat base rather than Le Verdon nearer the mouth. This town has the deepest port in France and lies close to the bustling metropolis of Royan, both with good harbour facilities.

The problem with Bordeaux is that the river keeps silting up, creating widespread shallows. This was made considerably worse during the war by the threat from river mines, dropped from aircraft over the less populated areas, which prevented dredging operations. Water depth had been a serious problem long before the Germans arrived and a rapid decrease of 2.5 metres from 9 to 6.5 metres, threatened to shut down the port to all but the smallest of ships. The large suction dredger *Pierre Lefort*, which had opened the channel leading up to the Normandie lock in St Nazaire, was hurriedly redeployed to create an adequate route through a kilometre-wide bar blocking the mouth. Strangely enough this impudent challenge to nature went without any immediate retribution and there were no signs of the deep water being filled in again by the sea nor by silt being washed down by the river. One and a half million cubic metres of sediment coming down each year could have made this quite a headache.

The decisive reason for choosing Bordeaux for a U-boat bunker, rather than ports nearer the sea, was that it could be built there in the shortest possible time. Work on the eleven-pen structure started in September 1941 and the first accommodation was available in January 1943, with the rest of the bunker being completed some five months later. The design differed from the other French bunkers inasmuch that it was erected directly over a firm, sandy base by merely placing a 4.5 metres thick concrete raft on top of the substrata. The individual pens were also a fair bit bigger than the other French bunkers so that they could accommodate both long-range IXD2 supply boats of Type XIV and the even larger minelayers of Type XB. The first mentioned had a length of almost 88 metres, which was a good deal longer than a Type VIIC at 66.5 metres. The supply tankers were the widest at a little over nine metres, which was three metres more than a Type VIIC. Since it was planned to develop Bordeaux as a special base for long-distance and supply boats, the bunker was built accordingly to accommodate any combination of submarine giants. It was not only the dimensions of the pens, but also the size of the oil stores which had to be made especially large. A Type XIV had bunkers for a staggering 635 tons of oil, while IXD2 had room for 442 tons. All this storage space was also placed under concrete with underground

Although the bunker building programme went ahead at an incredibly fast rate, there were a number of occasions when men with little experience in the intricacies of temperamental engines, cursed while the machinery ground away, spraying steam and threatening the workers with a ferocious hiss, but without making any apparent progress.

U178 passing through the lock at Bordeaux towards the U-boat bunker in the far distance and the nearly completed bunkered lock on the right. The pontoon-like structure towards the far right corner of the lock is a rotating bridge, allowing the road to pass over the lock and through the back of the bunker.

Konteradmiral Heinz-Eduard Menche, Chief of the Kriegsmarine Command in Bordeaux. Being a general naval base with considerable port activities meant that some of the larger places had special staffs for dealing with surface ships. Menche served in Bordeaux until June 1944 when he was given compassionate leave due to ill-health and two months later he was given an honourable discharge. The badge below the Iron Cross is the Wounded Badge, which would suggest that he has already seen some drastic action and is not in the best of health.

pipe connections to fill the boats while they were lying inside the pens. This was not unusual, but by no means universal. Keroman I and II in Lorient, for example, did not have such a facility. As with the other bunkers, the roof was made in several stages with an additional layer added later and, in this case, was somewhat different from the others in that almost all of the bomb catching grid over the top was completed by the time the German forces vacated the place at the end of the war.

Being located at the far end of a floating harbour, meant that the bunker had to be approached through one of two parallel locks, one of them 132 and the other 152 metres long. The shorter lock was 14 metres wide and the larger one 22 metres. The maximum size that could fit through them was 143 by 21 metres. This weak spot was reinforced by a bunkered lock, which was completed shortly before the Germans vacated the site but the protective dam around the building site had not yet been removed and therefore the lock was not used by U-boats.

There were numerous problems with the Gironde estuary as far as naval activities were concerned. Although the majority were overcome, the Kriegsmarine was left with a number of complaints, a few embarrassments and some disasters. The most annoying for operational U-boats was the time some of them had to wait before being given permission to enter the river. Nothing was more infuriating than coming home damaged after a long cruise and then not being able to get into port. This enforced wait out at sea was partly owing to the number of long-range boats coming home either well ahead of, or well behind, schedule so that the minesweeper escorts were not in place at the right time. At least U-boats had the advantage of being able to wait submerged, out of harm's way. Surface ships were not so lucky. Being a major seaport meant it was a destination for a number of auxiliary cruisers, their prizes and blockade breakers. The vast majority of these arrived in Bordeaux without too much trouble but a number didn't quite make it. One of the most tragic events occurred on 22 September 1940, when the 7,230GRT freighter *Tirranna* under Lt.z.S. (S.)

A view of the pen interior of the bunker at Bordeaux.

125

Waldmann and Lt.z.S. (S.) Mund, with 274 prisoners on board, was sunk by the British submarine *Tuna* (Lt Cdr Cavanagh-Mainwaring). *Tirranna* had been captured in the Indian Ocean by the auxiliary cruiser *Atlantis* under Kpt.z.S. Bernhard Rogge and her valuable cargo was dispatched to the Gironde. There was some confusion with radio codes but the crunch came when she was ordered to proceed at 10 knots on a straight course instead of her possible 17 and was then held up in the approaches to the Gironde for twelve hours, becoming a sitting duck for the British submarine. Two days later Cavanagh-Mainwaring achieved something of a coup by also sinking the catapult ship *Ostmark*. Unknown to most people at the time, this had far-reaching repercussions in the U-boat Command. Fearing that, sooner or later, U-boats would be lost, Dönitz had instigated a system whereby outward-bound boats had to broadcast a short signal when they reached the far western extremities of the Bay of Biscay so that escort ships could be alerted. Thanks to the breaking of the Enigma code, unknown to the German High Command, this signal was picked up and used by the secret submarine tracking room in London as an essential tool for identifying boats putting out to sea and thus made a noteworthy contribution to the Allies gaining the upper hand in the Atlantic.

At the same time as construction started on the U-boat bunker in Bordeaux, an autonomous Italian submarine command was founded in the city. The reason for this was that Dönitz did not want to drift into a position where the Italians would command German U-boats in the Mediterranean. Therefore he declined the offer to deploy their submarines in the Atlantic and instigated instead, the founding of this Italian Atlantic base. Known as Betasom (Beta = base, som from *sommergibili* meaning submarine), it was commanded for the first year by Admiral Angelo Parona, from September until December 1941 by Kapitän Polacchini and then for the remaining war period by Kapitän Grossi. In all, some 32 Italian U-boats operated out of Bordeaux. Although their integration into German wolf packs proved unsuccessful, they did score a number of remarkable individual successes.

Bordeaux also became the target for the so-called Cockleshell Heroes, a group of Allied commandos who paddled kayak canoes upriver to place magnetic mines on ships in the harbour, destroying a number of them.

An aerial view of Bordeaux, August 1942.

3
The Demolishers

COMING TO THE CRUNCH

Obtaining information about the effectiveness of Allied air raids and the nature of bombs can be somewhat frustrating. There is ample evidence to suggest that there was a deliberate cover-up to hide the futility of the bombing campaign and to steer historians away from the moral issue of 'atrocities' committed by the Allied air forces. The sad point about this killing and destruction is that it did not stop when the war ended, but continued for some time afterwards. Many port installations such as cranes, dry docks and even high water defences were demolished by the armies of occupation. There are a good number of photographs showing the devastation in the German dockyards, with captions proclaiming the efficiency of the bombing campaign. Yet there are also photographs of boats on stocks being inspected by British soldiers, without the massive damage in the background. Therefore, one must conclude that at least some of the destruction was the result of a concentrated demolition attempt on the ground, rather than raids by the air forces during the war.

The fact that the roofs were not thick enough had become apparent before the bunkers were completed and the matter was discussed with Hitler as early as August 1941. The really serious crunch came during the autumn of the following year, when heavier bombs were dropped on cities. Known as 'air mines' by the Germans, these were designed to create a heavy blast for knocking down apartment blocks. At the same time they were being used to kill masses of civilians while they hurried into the shelters. This killing was made worse by Allied broadcasts which pretended to come from the German side and warned people not to go into shelters because these were known to be the targets for the night. Consequently many civilians, women, children and old people were slaughtered in the streets as they fled

Raid on Wilhelmshaven.

127

The Allies' desperation which brought about such a grand scale of mass destruction after the war was not limited to the eradication of war relics. Dry docks, locks leading into floating harbours, factories and high water defences were also blown apart. This shows the large locks in Wilhelmshaven flying into the air after the war.

The building on the left is the old and obsolete signal tower by the Blücher Pier on the opposite side of the water from the Kilian bunker. The tangled remains of this pier are just visible after it had been demolished on order of the British authorities. The photographer was standing almost a kilometre away. A short while after pressing the camera's shutter release, he was thrown over by the pressure wave from the detonation.

from the terror. Although the air raid shelters were hardly touched on this occasion, it wasn't difficult to forecast that larger, concrete breaking bombs were likely to follow and plans were put in hand to increase the thickness of roofs over U-boat pens.

The Achilles heel of German bunker design was shown up during the summer of 1943, when a bomb detonated on top of the U-boat pen in St Nazaire, close to filled-in earlier bomb damage. Not only did this lift the plug out of the cone shaped hole, but it bent the iron supports in the roof. The corrugated iron sheeting prevented concrete from falling down and the damage was so slight that U-boat crews down below did not even notice it. Yet, the few centimetres of damage were measurable and gave the designers plenty of food for thought. There was no consensus of opinion about what should be done to withstand future attacks, but it was quite clear that a constant hail of detonations from small bombs was eventually going to shatter the roof. The old battering ram principle of the Middle Ages still applied. In the end, designers decided on three possible ways of overcoming the problem. the first being the obvious one of increasing the thickness of the roofs. The second was to place large stones over the top. Granite set in cement was suggested and this was tried out in Bergen and Brest, but the acquisition of such large blocks was considerably more problematic than making the same size defences out of concrete. The third and most promising suggestion was to add a concrete net or grid over the roof to deflect some of the blast. The idea was that this should lift detonations clear of the main roof and, at the same time, help to prevent armour piercing bombs from digging themselves into it. This, incidentally, was decided some time before the special 'Tallboys', or earthquake bombs, designed by Barnes Wallis, came into use.

One of the command bunkers in Wilhelmshaven during demolition. Some of this was quite intricate work and even old torpedo nets were hung over bunkers to protect windows in nearby buildings from flying concrete.

Left: The rear of the U-boat bunker at Brest, showing extensive bomb damage.

Below: The rear of Brest bunker with extensive bomb damage, but with the concrete apparently untouched.

Tallboys, fourteen of them, were dropped for the first time on Brest on 5 August 1944 and further raids continued throughout that month. Five of the first wave and a few more subsequent bombs hit the roof of the bunker, creating considerable holes. A couple even succeeded in piercing the concrete. Early British reports talk about U-boats being demolished and the Germans being driven from their stronghold. Yet, these hits occurred at a time when the bunker was already being evacuated and none of the three boats known to have been inside was damaged. (These were: U247 (Oblt.z.S. Gerhard Matschulat and later Heinrich Lehmann-Willenbrock), U953 (Oblt.z.S. Herbert Werner) and U963 (Oblt.z.S. Karl Boddenberg. Although these blasts did not damage U-boats, the raid had an enormous influence on the morale of the workers, who no longer remained working in the bunker when air raid sirens sounded, but raced frantically into the underground passages behind.

When looking at photographs of bunkers one cannot help but notice a wide variety of different fittings and doors. The reason why the majority of these were not standardised was that bitter experience caused the designs to be modified, even in the short period of time they had been installed. At the beginning of the war, it was thought best for storage and personnel bunkers to be fitted with the smallest number of tiny doors, but an incident where a cement mixer was blasted a considerable distance against an outward opening door changed this specification. The doors had been made to open outwards so that a bomb blast would force them tighter shut, rather than blow them open. On this occasion, a nearby, heavy cement mixer was forced tightly against the door, preventing anyone on the inside from opening the only exit. Fires erupting around the bunker probably suffocated everybody inside before slowly cooking them. Later, when it was realised what had caused the tragedy, designs were modified to create escape routes in times of emergency, but it was virtually too late to do anything about existing designs. Initially, towards the beginning of the war, there was still a considerable faith in the Luftwaffe repelling the majority of bombers, and even when this wavered, it was thought that anti-aircraft guns would keep a good many aircraft from their targets. However, this seems to have been a severe miscalculation. The 16-months period leading up to September 1944 saw Brest being attacked by well over 350 aircraft and only five of them were shot down. Therefore, the naval designers must have realised quite early on that they had to rely more or less entirely on the thickness and strength of their concrete bastions to defend the boats inside.

BUSTING THE BUNKERS

Although the Allied bombing campaign raged with severe intensity, U-boat bunkers did not come under direct threat until August 1944 when a new type of bomb was introduced. This device was first dropped in June, but 5 August marks the date when it was used against the concrete U-boat shelters. Up to that time some 80 raids, made up of over 3,300 bombers, had attacked Brest, the most northerly of the French U-boat bases. Both Lorient and St Nazaire had been bombed on thirty occasions each, while the southern ports of La Pallice and Bordeaux fared a little better, having been attacked fewer than half a dozen times. None of these raids scratched the bunkers, but reduced much of the towns to rubble.

The bitterness and intensity of this bombing campaign can be partly gauged by considering that one single raid (Operation Gomorrah) in July 1943 on Hamburg produced as many casualties as were lost in Britain during the entire war. This carnage, continuing unabated, became even worse after the summer of 1944, when the death toll of a single Allied raid on Dresden rose even higher than the catastrophic results from one of the atom bombs detonated over Japan. The onslaught against the civilian population

The results of an air raid on Wilhelmshaven. A reminder that there never can be victors in a war and many of those who claim victory are often nothing more than armchair warriors who had the privilege of avoiding the dreadful suffering. Wars are miserable and end with one side losing a little less than the other.

brought havoc to both German and French towns, reducing residential areas to rubble, in which people often died slow, agonising deaths or suffered the most appalling injuries. Yet, strangely enough, these constant attacks did very little to hamper the U-boat war; indeed, if anything, they caused the opposite to happen. The suffering inflicted on women, children and old people helped to create an atmosphere of defiance in which people worked harder than before. This made it possible to speed up the building of U-boats and provide a steady stream of enthusiastic volunteers at the recruiting offices.

The carnage created by the Allied bombing campaign has become one of the forgotten facets of the Second World War. It would appear that after the hostilities a deliberate attempt was made to eradicate the horrors of the bombing through a so-called re-education programme and confiscating both photographs and films of this most inhumane destruction. On top of that, German casualty records from first aid centres, veterinary treatment offices, air raid protection stations and so forth were destroyed during the immediate post-war years. Hans Brunswig, a senior fire-fighter in Hamburg who succeeded in salvaging some photographs and a few records from the bombings, found that his carefully assembled archive at fire headquarters was destroyed during the mid-1960's, immediately after he retired, leaving little trace of the large scale destruction and liquidation. The majority of his photos as well as moving film he made of the bombing

These pictures of Bergen on 20 April 1944 were thought to show the result of sabotage, but this appears to be false. The Norwegian historian Torstein Saksvik said that the German harbour master should never have allowed the former Dutch freighter Voorbode *so close to houses. 160 people were killed and about 5,000 injured when someone, probably accidentally, dropped a match to set off what could well have been 120 tons of dynamite. This massive detonation also caused the freighter* Rogaland *to go down in her berth.*

The Fink II bunker in Hamburg showing considerable bomb damage. The river Elbe is towards the right. The pens opened into the large basin of the Rüschkanal. Much of it has now been filled in, together with another canal to the right. The slipways of Deutsche Werft have also disappeared.

There seems to be a number of Tallboy or Grand Slam craters nearby. One of them is by the edge of the water by the moored ship, with two or three more towards the right of the bunker.

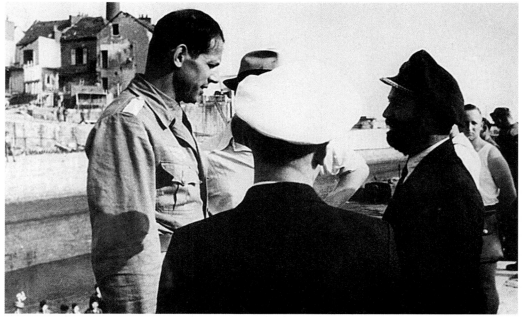

On the left is Korvkpt. Herbert Sohler, Chief of the 7th U-Flotilla, with ruins of St Nazaire in the background.

were confiscated by British authorities after the war and, despite several requests, have never been handed back, although some of the footage has appeared in a number of films.

The true extent of Allied operations against the German civilian population is part of the forgotten history of the war. Photographs showing airmen in smart uniforms with splendid medals, and emotional captions, suggest the devastating destruction had been a magnificent and joyous liberation. Indeed, younger generations, who did not witness the terror of the bombing, are often confronted with headings such as 'the friendly invasion', while adjectives like 'magnificent' and 'glorious' are used to describe the untold misery. Sadly, present day media concentrates, with incredible determination, on what the Germans did during the war but hardly ever considers the effects of the Allied bombing nor what was done to the Germans in the name of 'freedom'. This misery has created a wound that is yet to be healed.

The new bomb, mentioned earlier, appeared a few weeks after the D-Day invasion of Normandy and quickly became a vital tool in the Allied armoury for establishing a firm foothold on the continent. Mulberry harbours, consisting of huge floating concrete boxes, brought over for turning invasion beaches into temporary unloading areas, suffered considerable damage from a summer storm shortly after the armies landed. On top of this, the makeshift harbours were planned as an interim measure for the invasion and it was never intended that they should sustain the rapidly growing military force for any length of time. To overcome this weak link in the supply system, the American army

Much of Lorient was reduced to rubble by persistent air raids, forcing the German naval staff to move further away. Since there was an adequate vehicle pool and a reasonable quantity of fuel, this provided no great hardship for the navy, but created incredible suffering for the local population, many of whom lost their lives or all their belongings.

An official Citroën of the Naval Dockyard in St Nazaire has been blown from the ground on to the roof during an air raid. This shows the terrific pressure waves created by exploding bombs and clearly demonstrates that something as light as a person stands little chance and is likely to be hurled a long way. Yet there were times when relatively flimsy structures provided enough protection to save the lives of people sheltering behind them.

One of the major problems with the building of bunkers was the acquisition of raw materials. This shows one of many railway lines laid to the source of the supplies. The trouble with these was that they many lacked durable foundations, thereby putting the line very much at the mercy of the weather, and there were frequent cases where heavy steam engines pulling overloaded wagons sank into soft ground. Much credit for keeping such tracks open must go to the workers, who often reacted very quickly to prevent small incidents from becoming major disasters.

headed west for Cherbourg, where they hoped to establish their first supply port. Unfortunately, the harbour facilities there had been so thoroughly destroyed by earlier Allied bombing and by retreating Germans that some time was required before the installations could be repaired. Even the mole had been breached, allowing the full force of Atlantic gales to turn the relatively calm waters into a boiling fury.

Since it was more difficult for the Allied armies to make progress in the east, it was decided to head for Brest in the west, where the huge natural harbour offered the facilities needed to keep the invasion force running on schedule. The first American troops arrived there at about the same time as the new bomb came into service and it was used to soften up the resistance before allowing the army to advance through the still heavily defended ruins. Before going on to discuss the battle for the French U-boat bases, it might be advantageous to look at the development of this new concrete smashing bomb, which penetrated the roof of the U-boat pens in Brest on 5 August 1944, throwing the concept of reinforced protection into a totally new and somewhat horrifying dimension.

The story of the bomb started way back at the beginning of the war, when Barnes Neville Wallis, a classically eccentric engineer at the Vickers Armstrong works in Weybridge, wrote a 100-page paper on bombing. So far he had worked on airships and he was responsible for the revolutionary design of the Wellington bomber, but he had virtually no qualifications, nor any experience, in the subject of bombs. However, that did not prevent him from giving it considerable thought. Being somewhat of a pacifist, he could see no purpose in the wanton destruction, killing and maiming that had become the order of the day as a result of scattering small bombs over target areas, and he started looking for ways of crippling the enemy's war machine by striking a few well-aimed blows at crucial centres. Although no one in authority took him seriously at the time, his arguments could not be faulted. He stated quite simply that modern warfare depended on industry and that relied entirely on raw materials. Therefore, rather than hitting at armour and machinery, one should aim at shutting down the supply routes and the sources of the raw materials. To do this, he suggested using a large bomb, capable of penetrating deep into the ground to create an earthquake effect, the idea being that it would vibrate vulnerable industrial plant off its foundations, rather than blow down the buildings from above. He illustrated his thesis with first-hand experience, pointing to an air raid at the Vickers Armstrong works on 4 September 1940 when seven 220-pound bombs hit the main machine shop. Only 24 of 500 machines were damaged and all but two of these were repaired so that the production line was up and running again within a few days.

The problem for Barnes Wallis was that he lived some years before his contemporaries caught up with his way of thinking. He advocated that the air force should design bombs for the jobs which needed to be done and then build aircraft to carry them. Instead of subscribing to this logic, the higher commanders worked the other way round and built whatever bombs could be carried by existing aircraft. Not only were these small bombs ineffective against specific targets, but there was no way of aiming them at an exact spot. Therefore it was thought better to scatter a large number of small bombs rather than one big one.

In May 1943, Barnes Wallis became a national celebrity as a result of having designed the bouncing bomb which 617 Squadron of the Royal Air Force used to breach the Eder and Möhne dams during the famous Dambusters raid. Following this, the air staff dug out the paper on deep penetration or earthquake bombs and gave the go-ahead for some experimental trials. This resulted in the construction of three bombs and a little confusion with their names. First, Barnes Wallis used the letters DP to refer to 'deep penetration', but had to refrain from this because officialdom already claimed those initials to mean 'drill purpose'. Then the bomb was given the code name of Tallboy and virtually at the same time it was decided to build three of them as follows:

Tallboy S   (Small)   4,000 pounds for trial purposes.
Tallboy M   (Medium)   12,000 pounds for operational use.
Tallboy L   (Large)   22,000 pounds for operational use.

Later, Tallboy M became Tallboy while the larger version was called Grand Slam. On top of this, the scenario is made more confusing by another big bomb used by 617 Squadron of the RAF. This was a large, blunt-nosed object with fins at the rear called Blockbuster, which did not feature a great deal in the attacks against U-boat pens.

Both Tallboys and Grand Slams differed from existing bombs by having a thick shell made from precision-machined hardened steel of considerable thickness (1.5–4 inches or 3.5–10 centimetres) to withstand deformation as they smashed deep into the earth. One reason for producing two sizes was that they approached the limit which large bombers could carry for any distance. Barnes Wallis calculated that they should be dropped from a height of about 40,000 feet (12,000 metres), but the largest bomber, the Lancaster, could take them no higher than about 18,000 feet (5,500 metres) so compromises had to be made. The rocket-like bombs were travelling at about 320 kilometres or 200 miles per hour when they smashed into their target, making the Germans think that they were jet propelled. Their development coincided with another significant invention, that of a gyroscopically guided bomb sight, capable of aiming the huge bomb within Barnes Wallis's specifications. Accounts published during the first 20 years after the war suggest that this made a deadly combination by providing almost 100 per cent accuracy. Yet, official records would suggest that a good number were still way off target and some raids resulted in no damage despite 17 bombs having been dropped.

Tallboys were used for the first time during the night of 8–9 June 1944 against the Saumur railway tunnel, about half way between Tours and Angers, to prevent essential supplies from reaching the Normandy invasion area. Although released from only about 8–10,000 feet, the results were astonishing and instantly vindicated any remaining doubts about the effectiveness of Barnes Wallis's design. Official sources state that Tallboys were then used against U-boat pens in Boulogne, Ijmuiden, Pootershaven and Rotterdam, although there are no German records of these places having been used as submarine bases. But then, the Allied records relating to the period of the invasion are contradictory, making it exceedingly difficult to distinguish between errors, omissions and blatant lies from the propaganda systems.

Lifting such heavy weights to the ceiling of 18,000 feet was quite an aeronautical achievement. Especially when one bears in mind that experiments with high altitude flight were not conducted on any grand scale until after the war, when Barnes Wallis

A Tallboy bomb on display at the Brooklands Museum near Weybridge in Surrey. These enormous devices, with precision machined cases made from especially hard steel, were the first to cause serious damage to U-boat bunkers and some of them even pierced through seven metres of reinforced concrete.

helped the Vickers Armstrong works at Weybridge build a special wind tunnel in which machinery could be tested in extreme weather and pressure conditions. Incidentally, this incredible building can now be visited at the Brooklands Museum in Weybridge, home of the famous motor racing circuit and birthplace of British aviation. Not only did the Lancasters, which carried the bombs, have new powerful engines but also the trappings for coping with low pressure and extreme cold. This was such a specialised and difficult job that only two Royal Air Force Squadrons, No. 617 of Dambusters fame and later No. 9, ever achieved these goals.

Although Lancasters flying at extreme altitudes were the backbone of the squadrons, the aimers found that they were often so high that they could not see the target. After all, they were three and a half miles or five kilometres up in the sky and Europe rarely boasts ultra clear visibility. Consequently it was necessary to mark the target with brilliant flares before the bombers started their run-in. It was quickly discovered that the clumsy Lancasters were not suitable for this highly intricate task and twin-engined Mosquitoes were used to drop beacons from low altitude. This has led to considerable confusion and contradicting reports because many Germans saw the small bombers dive down, without noticing that a horde of larger planes was approaching much higher up. This is understandable inasmuch that the majority of observers were inside the air raid shelters by the time Tallboys started exploding and time delay fuses added even more to the confusion. The reason for these delay systems was to keep the target area clear of smoke until all the bombs had been released.

It would seem that the following raids with Tallboys and Grand Slams did take place:

Date	Bunker	Bombs dropped Number/Type		Hits on bunker
5 August 44	Brest	14	Tallboys	At least 5
6 August 44	Lorient	11	Tallboys	At least 1
9 August 44	La Pallice	12	Tallboys	2
12 August 44	Brest	8	Tallboys	At least 3
13 August 44	Brest	5	Tallboys	1
18 August 44	La Pallice	6	Tallboys	
12 January 45	Bergen	24	Tallboys	2
27 March 45	Valentin	2	Grand Slams	
30 March 45	Valentin	62	Disney Bombs*	1
4 April 45	Fink II	44	Disney Bombs*	0
9 April 45	Fink II	15	Tallboys	
		2	Grand Slams	6
19 April 45	Heligoland	22	Tallboys	
		6	Grand Slams	0

* Disney Bombs were American, rocket propelled bombs weighing about 4,500lbs and especially designed for penetrating concrete. Two of these would be strapped underneath the wings of a B-17 bomber.

A Grand Slam and the smaller trial bomb on display in the aircraft hangar at the Brooklands Museum near Weybridge in Surrey. A cylindrical 'Dam Buster' bomb, also designed by Barnes Wallis, can be seen towards the left, between the letter 'G' and the Grand Slam.

Children picking through the ruins of a house, Wilhelmshaven.

The side of Keroman I in Lorient after the first major air raid in October 1942, which made a considerable mess of the bunker's surroundings. Note that the anti-aircraft defences on the roof are not yet in place.

This view, looking northwards from above Krupp Germania Works in Kiel, shows the construction basin with the Konrad bunker, built over a dry dock. This bunker was used for building midget submarines of Type Seehund. The two U-boats in the right hand dry dock are U1227 and U2516. The building site for the Konrad bunker is just visible on the left. Originally this was also a dry dock, but was filled in to accommodate the masses of cement mixers and concrete pumps. In the far distance one can just make out the capsized hull of the pocket battleship and later heavy cruiser Admiral Scheer.

Both the bunkers Valentin near Bremen and Nordsee III on Heligoland were bombed with Tallboys and probably also with Grand Slams after the end of the war, causing some additional damage to roofs and interiors.

It must be pointed out that hitting the target was not the primary object of the exercise. Barnes Wallis had calculated that more damage would be done if the bomb hit the ground by the side, so that it could penetrate deep into the ground to rupture the structure from below. However, the air staff could not be prevented from trying this new invention against hard surfaces such as the roofs of U-boat pens. The results were literally shattering and are best described from the German point of view. Several documents in the U-Boot Archiv make this possible. There is also the book *Iron Coffins* by Herbert Werner, which has received quite damning reviews because parts of it were exaggerated and other parts have been disputed, but his description of the last days in Brest match other, earlier reports and remains fascinating.

Brest had been in the boiling pot since D-Day on 6 June 1944, with many boats going out to challenge the invasion supply routes and being sunk en route. A new book by Innes McCartney has shown that the official histories of this period are somewhat incorrect in giving so much credence to the aircraft of Operation Cork which was supposed to have blocked off the western approaches of the Channel. Through diving and looking at wrecks, McCartney has established that a good number of U-boats are lying a long way from their reported sinking positions and far more boats than previously thought had reached the invasion beaches off Normandy to be sunk by ships of the Royal Navy. By the time the RAF launched the first attacks with Tallboys against the U-boat pens in Brest, the majority of boats from there had either been evacuated or sunk. Those remaining in the bunker were undergoing repairs and U963 was having a schnorkel fitted.

The evacuation of Brest was considered important because both specialised personnel and equipment such as radar sets and parts for the new acoustic torpedo could be salvaged for future use if they could be moved further south to La Pallice, from where there were still reasonable opportunities for making the increasingly perilous cross-country journey to Germany. The journey from Brest to La Pallice entailed a submerged passage of about 440 kilometres, meaning it was necessary to surface several times for charging batteries. Although incredibly hazardous, with a number of boats being sunk, there was the one slight advantage that Asdic did not work terribly well in shallow water and therefore U-boat crews were willing to make the sacrifice, rather than fall into enemy hands. In many ways, looking back at that chaotic situation, it seems astonishing that Brest was defended so well and that so many men gave their lives to make it possible for the last U-boats to get out to sea. Much of this credit must go to a paratroop regiment which had taken over the defence of the ruins and was responsible for keeping the United States army at bay for a considerable period of time.

U953, U963 and U256 were definitely still in Brest at the time of the first Tallboy attack. Karl-Heinz Marbach of U953, who had received the Knights Cross on 22 July, and a large proportion of his crew took the BdU Special train to Germany for home leave and Karl Boddenberg of U963 was on leave as well when advancing United States troops made their return impractical. Herbert Werner, whose U415 had been mined in front of the bunker in Brest on 14 July 1944, while he was not on board, was given command of U953. At the same time, the first watch officer of this boat, Oblt.z.S. Werner Müller, was ordered to take command of U963. The decisive reason for this appointment being that there was no one else in Brest with schnorkeling experience. The third boat, U256, was later taken to Norway by the commander of the 9th U-Flotilla, Korvkpt Heinrich Lehmann-Willenbrock.

5 August 1944, one day after Werner Müller's 24th birthday, was a bright, sunny, summer's day when the air raid sirens caused men to scatter into the bunker. Müller, however, shot off in the other direction, to seek shelter in the underground passages leading up to the naval school on top of the rocky cliffs. Looking up, he saw aircraft approach at an altitude of about 500 metres. Thinking this was the core of the attack, he quickly made his way deep underground but had not gone very far when he was struck by a violent tremor of an earthquake. The experience was weird and totally unexpected. The anti-aircraft gunners and duty firemen found the noise was hardly deafening, nor were there any great sheets of flames which had accompanied so many of the previous big bombs. Instead, it felt very much as if the men's chests were being hit with

This picture was taken from a position by the top of Kilian's side wall with the southern submarine pen in the foreground and the remains of the accommodation block lying in what was the northern submarine pen. The sand has been washed onto the site to convert it to dry land for making into a new part of the harbour.

Right: Peering into the massive opening of the Valentin bunker is indeed an awe-inspiring experience, showing a cavernous hall of immense proportions. The pitch-black water and the crying of numerous crows gave the whole scene a most eerie feeling. The gangway towards the right of the picture gives some indication of size, but without some more definite comparison, it is difficult to appreciate the vastness of this overpoweringly high bunker.

Below: Looking east from the central supporting wall towards the back of the Kilian bunker in Kiel. The vast crumpled roof has slipped off the wall and is lying in the water towards the right, while the workshop block at the back survived the demolition, to remain standing defiantly by what is now the edge of a scrap metal yard. The thin rods supporting a rope in the foreground mark the edge of the route which was used for guiding people around the ruins.

One of the ships sunk in Bordeaux harbour by the Cockleshell Heroes, who paddled up the river Garonne to attach limpet mines to ships lying at anchor in the tidal part of the harbour.

sledgehammers. Despite the chaos, most of the U-boat men described the experience as fascinating and curious rather than frightening. Having got used to prolonged depth charge attacks within the dark and stinking confines of a rocking submarine made this a considerably milder and even somewhat exotic experience, which lasted no more than about fifteen minutes, considerably shorter than the usual prolonged depth charge hunt.

Once the all-clear sounded, a number of men made their back out to see what had happened. The anti-aircraft gunners on the roof had gone without trace and the remains of their bodies were later recovered from the surroundings. By the side of the bunker was a huge cone shaped hole, large enough to accommodate a detached family house. Debris was strewn around over a vast area, but there was little other damage and much less chaos than the men had got used to from the carpet bombing of many smaller detonations. Two Tallboys had hit the bunker roof to blast massive cone shaped holes in the concrete. Earlier reports stated that these two had penetrated the roof and detonated inside the bunker, but this appears to be untrue. What happened was that the bomb smashed its way through part of the thick concrete roof, having just missed the section with the bomb-catching beams. The detonation then blasted the concrete below it down on to a minesweeper, blowing a metre diameter hole in the roof. At the same time. the usual cone shaped depression was excavated towards the top. None of the three U-boats in the bunker were harmed, nor was the minesweeper immediately below the explosion. Most of the damage was caused by concrete falling on the ship, rather than by the direct blast. Earlier reports of the bomb having pierced the roof and having detonated inside probably originated from the German description of having felt a massive pressure wave as it travelled through the bunker. Ships out in the harbour fared considerably worse, however, one tanker was turned over, to lie keel-up by the side of the breakwater.

Although relatively little material damage was done to the German war machine. the attack had a fantastic effect upon the men. So far, the bunker had been considered impregnable-to such an extent that a number of withdrawing army troops had taken up residence. Now, suddenly, this invincible stronghold had become a deadly liability. Instead of seeking out the U-boat bunker as a safe place of refuge, men scurried from it to find shelter in the underground passages. It wasn't difficult to guess that the bunker was the main target and everybody knew that the thick roof was no longer going to protect them.

The supply ship Tannenfels *sinking in Bordeaux harbour after a daring attack by British commandos.*

The naval school, at the top of the hill, suffered as well, but having been built with a reinforced concrete core covered in bricks meant that the damage was not as severe as it might have been, had it been an all-brick construction. Once again, it was not the material damage but the demoralising effect which was worse, with men not wanting to sleep there any longer. However, this hardly concerned the U-boat crews, who were on the verge of pulling out, and the rest of the Germans soon fell into American hands to become prisoners of war.

The situation in Germany became considerably more desperate and bombing raids there increased both in severity and intensity until a few days before the cease-fire came into effect at 0800 hours on Saturday, 5 May 1945. It is now difficult to ascertain from the number of contradicting reports how many, if any, U-boats were sunk by enemy action while inside bunkers. It seems highly likely that all the wrecks found after the war were scuttled by their own crews. A raid on Fink II in Hamburg may have resulted in one, perhaps two casualties. The one certainty is, of course, U4708 in the Kilian bunker (Kiel), which has already been mentioned. That is not to say that the other German

Wreck of the Kilian bunker, seen from the Kiel Förde towards the end of the twentieth century. Shuttering in the foreground has been put in place so that the entire area can be filled with sand to become a new harbour. The bunker's accommodation and office block, with a number of small steel-shuttered windows, is visible towards the left, lying at a somewhat precarious angle. The walls on both sides of the southern submarine pen are towards the right, while the other, northern pen was situated between this and the accommodation block. The building in the background, between the two upright walls, is what is left of the workshops at the rear of the bunker.

The accommodation and office block which once stood by the side of the Kilian bunker seen from the remains of the workshops.

bunkers were left in peace, but several attempts at putting the major shipyard of Blohm und Voss in Hamburg out of action failed because the bombers found the target obscured by thick clouds. The reason for concentrating on Blohm und Voss was that it had become a major assembly line for the new class of electro-boat of Type XXI. The curious point about these repeated failures to find this target is that it is located on a relatively narrow and distinct peninsula in the river Elbe, and early reports about British airborne radar stated that this equipment was exceptionally good at distinguishing between water and land. But how good can it have been? In addition to the shipyard of Blohm und Voss, the area offered another exceedingly attractive target in the form of the petroleum harbour and a refinery nearer Harburg, towards the south. Yet, finding these places covered with clouds made the aircraft abandon their primary objective and dump their bombs on the city of Hamburg instead, killing somewhere in the region of 300 people.

The naval installations in Kiel were not let off so lightly. Finding the area clear of cloud, some 600 Lancasters with a handful of Mosquito pathfinders plastered the dock installations on the eastern side of the Förde. This was indeed a night to remember and it is only thanks to a goodly number of well-built air raid shelters that there were so few casualties. In fact, the official number of 81 civilians killed hardly reflects the immense damage done to the shipyard installations and to shipping in the harbour. The heavy cruiser and earlier pocket battleship, *Admiral Scheer*, the heavy cruiser *Admiral Hipper*

A view of the Vulkanhafen with Elbe II in the corner of the basin on the right. The fact that there is virtually no visible damage would suggest that this photograph was taken early during the war. Most of the buildings have something to do with shipbuilding and the main slips can be seen at the bottom towards the left. They are covered with a metal framework holding a multitude of travelling gantry types of cranes.

The caption on the back of this photograph says this is U345 under Oblt.z.S. Ulrich Knackfuss, but that boat was damaged during an air raid in Germany and never got as far as France. The only place where U-boats could be hauled out of the water and onto the land, as is shown in this picture, was at Lorient, suggesting that the bunker on the left is Keroman I. (Looking in the other direction one would see the earlier Dombunkers.*) The boat looks rather worse for wear and in need of a dry dock.*

and the light cruiser *Emden*, as well as a number of U-boats were lying in the basins around the Germania works, now HDW-Kiel. Having come back from the eastern Baltic with masses of refugees, the death toll could have been much higher, had the majority of these people not moved away from the area or found refuge in the air raid shelters. *Hipper* and *Emden* were demolished beyond use and *Admiral Scheer* capsized to lie keel-up in her berth. The offices as well as the workshops of the shipyard were reduced to a flaming inferno and rubble.

This raid was so intense that even the heavy doors of the Kilian bunker were torn off their rails to be thrown on top of U4708, lying inside the bunker. One eye witness report states that this caused a gash in the pressure hull through which water then entered, while another account states that a bomb detonating on the far shore created a high wave which washed over the kilometre wide Förde to flood down through open hatches. Whatever happened, it was dark and the survivors inside the bunker were not in a position to prevent this Type XXIII from sinking at its berth. It has already been mentioned that U170 was made fast in the same box, but her commander, Oblt.z.S. of the Reserve Hans-Gerold Hauber, had ordered the crew to rig the boat for diving by keeping hatches and bulkheads tightly shut. Consequently, U170 survived the onslaught. When the men peered out after the biggest of the blasts, the duty crew inside the central control room found themselves in total darkness. The raid had been a terrifying experience, with enough near-misses and direct hits on the bunker to make everything shake. It was only the flames of ships lying further out in front of the bunker that provided any light until the sound of aircraft faded away and men switched on powerful searchlights. Sweeping the basin in the direction of cries for help, they discovered an immediate shortcoming in the bunker design. A number of people had been blasted into the water and were having great problems finding their way out again. The walls rose vertically and the few iron ladders were difficult to locate in the confused darkness. Concentrating first on the splashes in the water, it took a while for men of U170 to realise that their smaller neighbour, U4708, had vanished without trace. Taut mooring ropes disappearing into the water suggested that it had gone down rather than out, and then someone spotted the tall conning tower lying sideways, supported by the bigger hull. This meant a number of dangerous dives had to be undertaken to ascertain that the underwater parts, such as rudders and hydroplanes, had not been damaged. But it was not so urgent because there were no prospects of moving the boat in the immediate future. Instead, U170 was put to good use as an emergency power plant for supplying electricity. The boat was later moved to Horten in Norway, where the crew surrendered.

Having fished men from the water, the few survivors inside the bunker realised that they were lucky to be alive. The anti-aircraft gunners on the roof had either died or vanished and there was no sign of life around them. The flickering light from numerous fires indicated that the whole eastern shore was in ruins.

Later in the war, despite British forces being almost within walking distance of Bremen, the Royal Air Force mounted another massive attack against the large bunker, Valentin, near Farge. A speaker in the House of Commons suggested to the Honourable Members that this assault was essential because the Atlantic campaign was about to be vigourously restarted with new U-boats! This was almost certainly nothing more than an excuse to try out Barnes Wallis's new, heavier Grand Slam bombs to see whether they were also capable of piercing reinforced concrete. During the last days of the war, considerable resources were devoted to bombing the empty and incomplete bunker at Farge, causing a great deal of damage, and this continued long after the armistice had been signed. People living in the area were evacuated from their homes before the site was used as bombing target.

After the war, the Allied armies of occupation decided that U-boat bunkers in Germany should be removed so that they could never be used again, and explosive experts were sent in to demolish them. The bunkers at Kiel and Fink II in Hamburg were brought down with whatever explosives were found still to be stockpiled, but this store was exhausted by the time they turned their attention to the old Elbe II bunker in the Vulkanhafen. Having achieved very little there with blasting, the job was put out to tender for German firms to complete. The strength and quantity of the concrete can be gauged from the fact that three firms went bankrupt trying to remove it (see page 74). In

The Kilian bunker in Kiel photographed shortly after the initial demolition by British Royal Engineers. At this stage a considerable effort was put in first to salvage iron from the ruins and then to knock down some of the remaining walls.

the end, the stubborn remnants were left in situ, where they have remained ever since. The last firm to go to the wall as a result of taking on the demolition challenge was so short of cash that it devoted its remaining resources to removing iron from the roof to sell on the scrap metal market. At the same time, the engines and conning towers of boats still lying inside were removed. It is tragic that this happened as late as the mid-1960s, by which time the three Type XXI U-boats inside the bunker had aged enough to have distinct historic value and could have formed the core of a magnificent museum and memorial. The only bunker outside Germany to be demolished after the war was Bruno at Bergen in Norway. This was done because an earlier attack with Tallboys had left the structure unsafe. Otherwise, France has retained most of its heritage of U-Boat bases virtually intact, only German bunkers being earmarked for destruction.

THE RAID ON ST NAZAIRE

On 27 March 1942, British combined operations launched a seaborne attack on St Nazaire with the primary objective of putting the huge 'Normandie' lock out of action,

Bunker Bruno in Bergen was the only one outside Germany to be demolished after the war. The reason for this was that one of the main supporting walls was blown out of true during a bombing raid, leaving the entire structure somewhat unsafe. However, despite this concerted effort, the demolition only destroyed part of the concrete structure and the remains are still visible. This set of pictures was taken after the war, during the demolition process.

that being the only dry dock on the Biscay coast capable of holding the battleship *Tirpitz*. *Bismarck*, of course, had already been sunk by that time. The plan was to discourage the Germans from employing her as a merchant raider in the Atlantic. This combined operations assault has been documented exceedingly well with excellent photographs in the magazine *After the Battle*, issue No. 59 as well as in other books. Therefore it seems superfluous to go into too many details here, other than to add the observation that it appears strange that no effort was made to block the other two locks and thus prevent U-boats from using the bunker in the floating harbour. Incidentally, 'Normandie Lock' is not an official name to be found on maps, but the huge basin was especially constructed for building the passenger liner with that name and seems a better identification for people who do not know the area.

Since this was the only major attack on a U-boat base by landing troops, it may be of interest to look at the raid from the German point of view. This is possible because, as has already been mentioned, Herbert Sohler (Chief of the 7th U-Flotilla) has left his personal reminiscences in the Deutsches U-Boot-Museum.

March 1942 was an exceptionally busy period, with a large number of boats running into St Nazaire. Consequently the Commander-in-Chief, Admiral Karl Dönitz, appeared several times from his headquarters at Kerneval near Lorient to

The British destroyer Campbeltown *after the fatal explosion which destroyed the gates of the large Normandie Lock at St Nazaire. It seems likely that the anti-torpedo net was there before the destroyer arrived and it merely barged its way through these floating defences.*

The U-boat Chief, Admiral Dönitz in the centre while visiting the Italian Submarine Command Betasom in Bordeaux. The Italians might be excused for hanging the German flag the wrong way round, but there are a good number of photographs in the Deutsches U-Boot-Museum showing the Kriegsmarine having made the same mistake.

Guards on the Italian submarine base at Bordeaux.

welcome crews and to hand out awards. It was after one of these occasions, while officers were settling into armchairs in the mess, that Dönitz suddenly proposed the question, "Sohler, what are you going to do if the English arrive here one day?" There was no need to fish for an answer. The problem had been spinning through everybody's mind for about a year, ever since the 7th U-Flotilla first arrived in St Nazaire. A discussion with the staff and with other experts produced the conclusion that such an event was highly unlikely. The approaches to the port were exceedingly shallow, with so little depth that a narrow channel had to be especially dredged to get the passenger liner, *Normandie*, out of her building dock and that single route was still the only way into the comparatively huge floating harbour. To make matters even more difficult for potential attackers, the approach ran close to the cliffs, where a French coastal battery had fallen into German hands in such good condition that it was immediately manned by Kriegsmarine gunners. In addition to this, they had also placed a number of additional 88mm guns in strategic places. Despite these defences, Sohler had designed a special plan to be put into operation as soon as the appropriate alarm was sounded. This involved evacuating U-boat personnel and preparing the boats in the bunker for destruction. Dönitz had tossed the question out more as a conversation piece, rather than a serious enquiry, since he

Aircraft were discouraged from low-level attacks with anti-torpedo netting in front of vulnerable pens and a set of barrage balloons above the bunkers. Although quite innocuous looking, both these required a considerable number of men with vital equipment to keep them fully operational and to prevent these defences from interfering with U-boat movements.

knew full well that Sohler was the type who left nothing to chance. Therefore it seemed unnecessary to even check his procedures.

Dönitz departed at about 2200 hours to be driven back to Kerneval near Lorient by his personal assistant, Stabsgefreiter F. Büsching, while the 7th U-Flotilla officers took advantage of the party-like atmosphere by allowing a few more drinks to flow. Sohler left them in high spirits at about 2300 hours. An hour later he was woken up by the telephone with the message that the English were landing at St Nazaire. The Germans at that time hardly ever used the term 'British' and referred to Scots, Irish and Welsh as 'English' as well. Sohler reacted instantaneously with, 'You are under the influence of alcohol. Get yourself relieved at once.' But the voice on other end was adamant, assuring Sohler that the news had just been received from the port commander. Sohler still wasn't convinced and asked to be connected with him. The report was indeed critical. Sohler was told that half of the port and half of the town were already in British hands as a result of an onslaught by a couple of cruisers with a number of destroyers and torpedo boats having landed assault troops.

Sohler ran into the officers' mess shouting that the English had landed in St Nazaire and the base was to be evacuated immediately. A wave of laughter erupted from the late night revellers and it took a while before Sohler convinced them that he was deadly serious. He ordered the most senior commander, Korvkpt Ernst-August Rehwinkel of U578, to take charge of the immediate evacuation of U-boat crews to La Roche Bernard, about 25 kilometres away, and to report when they arrived there. Trained U-boat men were in such short supply that there were strict standing orders preventing them from becoming involved in land fighting. Having got his men on the move, the next step was to break the news to Dönitz, who had probably only just arrived back in Kerneval. The Lion's first question was, "What is happening to my U-boats?" Sohler couldn't provide an answer, but assured him that he would be in the bunker as soon as possible and report back from there.

The sharpness of Dönitz's tone quickly mellowed when his staff told him that less than twelve hours earlier, Kptlt Gerd Kelbling of U593 had reported a flotilla of three destroyers and several torpedo boats far out in the Bay of Biscay. No action was taken at the time because it was thought that they had been laying mines and were then on their way back to Britain. It would appear that they were first sighted at 0720 and quickly forced U593 into the cellar. The strange thing was that the subsequent depth charge attack was very much a half-hearted affair, nowhere near as severe as the baptism of fire the boat had received a few days earlier in the Atlantic. Knowing U593 had no weapon for sinking fast, shallow draught warships with alert lookouts, it was safest to remain deep and out of the way until the destroyers lost interest in the U-boat. This was U593's first voyage and caution was still very much the order of the day. Kelbing surfaced towards late morning to report the sighting. Later, when he ran into St Nazaire, it became obvious what his lookouts had seen. The British ships had not been keen on hunting U593 because they had more audacious plans to occupy their minds. It also became clear why they were flying the German flag before hoisting the White Ensign and driving the U-boat away. Twenty months later, Kelbing got his own back on

Above: The Eastern wet box of Elbe II bunker shortly before it was totally demolished at the beginning of the twenty-first century. The beginnings of the new, growing container port, which now covers this site, can be seen in the background.

Right: The workshop area at the back of the Kilian bunker in Kiel. The original thick, outside wall is visible towards the right, while a thinner wall, leading from this section into the boat mooring pens, can be seen towards the left. This also shows clearly, the staggering thickness of the roof. The bunker itself was very much higher than suggested by this picture, which has been taken from the first floor.

one of these annoying destroyers, HMS *Tynedale*. On 12 December 1943, at almost exactly the same time as he first sighted the group in the Bay of Biscay, he torpedoed her in the Mediterranean.

Sohler had hardly reached St Nazaire when he heard and saw gunfire as well as a brilliant display of searchlights illuminating the black sky. The first major problem occurred when he started making his way through the suburbs. There he was confronted with such a mass of crossfire that it looked suicidal to continue through it. Everybody was seemingly shooting at everybody else without waiting to find out whether they were friend or foe. It looked as if anything which moved was likely to be blown to pieces or at least raked with bullets, making the last few kilometres more than a foolhardy undertaking. Surveying the scene and wondering how it would be best to proceed, Sohler found himself being overtaken by three lorries with well-armed men from the Naval Anti-Aircraft Brigade. The order to clear a path to the bunker was complied with instantly and it was not long before the flotilla chief could convince himself that everybody in the bunker had carried out the emergency defence plan and prepared the boats for destruction.

Both the Fink II bunker and the remains of Deutsche Werft have been levelled. Today the area is occupied by a number of small industries centred around yachting rather than submarines. There are still a few clues that this was once home to some form of heavy industry: the remains of high tension electricity cables are hidden in what looks like a parkland landscape.

The front of Elbe II showing the demolished western wall and sloping roof with the three submarines of Type XXI still underneath. Getting into the bunker from the front was a problem but there was easy access from the back, then being used for storage by Howaldtwerke-Deutsche Werft. This part of the quay was used by the salvage firm Harms, hence the abundance of heavy lifting gear lying around.

A shot through the wire netting of the west gate, showing the underside of the sloping roof. The grave of the three U-boats is situated towards the left of this picture.

Two hours after that first telephone call to Dönitz, Sohler succeeded in obtaining a connection from the bunker to Kerneval to tell the boss that everything was running according to plan. A small number of men, armed with only light weapons, were guarding the bunker. Confusion was still prevailing when an army major reported that he had surrounded the town and would reinstate German control as soon as daylight made further progress possible. Sohler was not the type to be easily excited, but on this occasion he flew off the handle, telling his army counterpart that submarines were the only weapon with which they could hit at Britain and more must be done to protect the U-boats in the bunker. Hanging around for daylight was not good enough. Instant action was required. Despite warning the major that he could face court martial if he did not launch his counterattack immediately, the army remained firmly entrenched along the outskirts of the town, leaving the navy to defend the base the best it could with the light weapons at its disposal.

When daylight did eventually make it possible to see what was going on, men in the bunker were faced with the macabre sight of many dead bodies strewn around the harbour area. The purpose of the attack was not immediately clear, although it was not hard to guess that the destroyer *Campbeltown*, lying firmly wedged in the Normandie dock, was there for the purpose of shutting it down. With things apparently quiet on all fronts and with the first streaks of daylight illuminating the eastern horizon, Sohler gave permission for U-boat crews and workers to return. At the same time, he drove around the dock basin to inspect the lock, which appeared to have been the main focus of the attack. Despite several guards having been given strict instructions not to allow anyone onboard the *Campbeltown*, they could hardly hold back Sohler and his entourage, with its abundance of 'scrambled egg' on their caps. The destroyer had already been searched for explosives, but none were found, so everything looked clear and straightforward, without anything preventing further U-boat operations.

Sohler had hardly left the *Campbeltown* and was only a few metres away when a massive explosion erupted, hurling parts of the destroyer high into the air. The guards, as well as about a hundred workers inspecting the ship, were killed instantly. Sohler only just survived, but the noise of the blast damaged his hearing for some time. The big questions also ringing in his ears were: how did the British manage to get into St Nazaire and why did the inspection by German explosive experts not find any evidence before the massive detonation that ripped the *Campbeltown* apart? The first obstacle, of crossing the shallows, was overcome by mounting the raid on a high spring tide during an exceptionally dark, moonless night. The invading flotilla of specially selected, shallow draught boats was guided by at least one experienced French Loire pilot and, in addition to this, the British had some extraordinarily good intelligence, answering the challenge from coastal lookouts with the correct password. Despite this, the commander of the naval artillery unit, Kpt.z.S. Karl Conrad Mecke, was woken to be informed that major units were entering the Loire estuary. It was Mecke's personal intuition, or whatever, which made him order the guns to open fire at the unannounced visitors. This single move did more than anything else to rumble the well-disguised attack and one wonders what might have happened had Mecke not taken this grave decision upon

The rear of the bunker at St Nazaire in 2000. The railway lines around the bunker have almost all vanished and replaced by coach and car parks. The bridge is an inclined plane to allow both people and vehicless access to the roof from where splendid views can be obtained. Compare this with the view on the top of p. 108.

himself. As it turned out he was correct and later received the Knights Cross for his cool handling of such an overpowering situation.

This daring British raid was not the end of the matter. Two days later, the Prien Barracks in St Nazaire, where land-based personnel of the 7th U-Flotilla were accommodated, came under fire from surrounding houses. The response was swift and effective. Well-armed groups quickly surrounded the hot spots, captured a good number of resistance fighters and quickly transferred them to a prison camp at Savenay. Sohler had just arrived in the mess at La Baule, some ten kilometres away, when the telephone informed him about the noisy intrusion. Hurrying back to his car, he found Heinrich Lehmann-Willenbrock of U96 offering to accompany him to the troublespot. Sohler thanked him for his support, but reminded Lehmann-Willenbrock that the strictest of orders prevented U-boat men from being involved in land fighting. Lehmann-Willenbrock replied that he had just been relieved of his command to become the chief of the 9th Flotilla in Brest, therefore the instructions didn't apply to him any longer. Although a generally lucky person, this time he was not rewarded for his efforts. Instead, he received an injury in his foot for his troubles. Once again, the arrival of troops in St Nazaire did not alleviate the immediate situation and it appeared as if everybody was shooting at everybody else without waiting to find out whether they were friend or foe.

The following morning, Dönitz received a phone call from Generalfeldmarschall Gerd von Rundstedt (Supreme Commander-in-Chief, West), complaining about the manner in which the navy had responded to the attack. Apparently the defenders had gone wild, shot indiscriminately at civilians and destroyed the trust of co-operation which had been built up over the past months. Dönitz, who still had not heard any intimate details, told the field marshal that he had trained his men to defend themselves if they were attacked and then telephoned Sohler to find out what had happened. Hearing Sohler's explanation, he was satisfied that the navy had repelled the onslaught without interference from superior commands and the matter settled down.

Everybody, including Hitler himself, appeared content with the manner in which the navy had defended its base, but later the Führer was somewhat dismayed to read in both Swiss and Swedish newspapers that the British raid had achieved its objective of putting the Normandie lock out of action and thus denied the Germans the only dry dock on the Biscay coast capable of holding the mighty battleship *Tirpitz*. As a result, he sent his naval adjutant, Kpt.z.S. Karl-Jesko von Puttkamer, to St Nazaire with instructions to find out what had happened. Following this, Hitler ordered the naval commanders, who should have prevented the onslaught, to be placed before a special court martial under

Looking from the back of the Hornisse bunker towards the river Weser. The protruding walls are clearly visible, indicating that the bunker would have been much longer had it been completed.

After the war the Allied forces were not so concerned with the preservation of naval buildings around the dockyard and, despite these being able to provide essential housing for masses of homeless refugees, attempts were made to demolish them with explosives. A section of the bunker has been blown out to show the spiral interior as well as the thick walls. The fact that the majority of these bunkers survived the war, to be demolished afterwards, would suggest that the circular design with cone shaped roof worked exceptionally well.

the chairmanship of Field Marshal Gerd von Runstedt. Runstedt had mellowed considerably by the time this started and he opened the proceedings by apologising for having to conduct such a trial, but pointed out that he was also obeying orders direct from the Führer.

It quickly transpired that everybody along the chain of unfortunate events had informed their superiors that the defences were wholly inadequate, but the military high command did not allocate the necessary resources because the officers there also considered such an intrusion to be highly unlikely. So, the court martial turned into a case of too little, too late, in terms of taking the necessary steps for preventing further raids. However, there was nothing in the armoury reserves to create the forces necessary to guard all the weak links in the access routes to the German bases and it was very much a case of moving vital parts, such as communications and command centres, away from vulnerable positions near the coast. Worst hit was Dönitz's U-boat operations room, which had been established in a purpose-built bunker next to his requisitioned house at Kerneval near Lorient. Although well protected from bombs, it was right on the seafront and made an excellent target for a bunch of well-motivated commandos landing from small boats on a dark night. One such attack could put the entire Atlantic operations at risk. Dönitz had already been ordered to move further inland, but not wanting to distance himself from the commanders at sea, he ensured that the relocation process proceeded as slowly as possible. Now, thanks to this raid on St Nazaire, he was suddenly faced with the reality of having to move rather faster.

The court martial also established that the British force consisted of the old destroyer *Campbeltown*, two smaller destroyers and 16 fast launches, carrying 621 men, of which just over 260 were specially trained commandos. Only four of these units succeeded in making their way back to England. Therefore the emergency plans, with the limited resources devised by the naval personnel, had worked exceedingly well.

The German Navy in Norway and France

The German assault on Norway and Denmark was launched on 9 April 1940 and the invasion of Holland, Belgium and France followed a month later, with the famous Dunkirk evacuation of the British Expeditionary Force taking place between 27 May and 4 June. Brest, the first of the French bases to fall, was evacuated from the end of July to early September 1944, while Norway remained in German hands until the end of the war. This meant that the French Atlantic bases were used by the Kriegsmarine for a period of just over four years and Norwegian ports remained operational for almost five years. A comparatively short period, when one considers the vast building projects undertaken in those far-flung locations.

To make use of the opportunities created by the availability of foreign ports, the German navy had to deal with the following main tasks:

1. Establish harbours and anchorages for U-boats and surface ships.
2. Provide accommodation for U-boat crews and crews from other small boats, such as E-boats and motor minesweepers. (Large surface ships remained operational while lying in port with anti-aircraft guns manned and crews lived in their usual quarters aboard the ship. Life in small boats and submarines, on the other hand, was rather Spartan and better land-based quarters were provided while these were in port.)
3. Provide routine maintenance, repair and medical facilities.
4. Provide the normal supportive naval services for operational units, such as minesweepers, escorts and pilots etc.
5. Establish defences and protection for all the supporting services and vessels in harbours.
6. Create a supply system as well as the necessary backup to keep both operational and supportive systems functioning effectively.

As might be expected, the naval administration in both Norway and France started on a reasonably simple, makeshift level and then quickly mushroomed into a complicated network. The whole process of living and working in foreign countries was not static and constantly changed as far-flung theatres of war influenced naval support activities. For example, until the spring of 1941, most of the fuel in France was supplied by railway tankers but then the invasion of Russia dictated that these wagons should be transferred to the Eastern Front and the French ports had to be supplied by other means. This often entailed sailing from Germany through precarious coastal waters of the English Channel and involved considerable upheaval by requiring escorts, minesweepers and, at times, air support. To make matters more complicated, anyone studying this network will quickly be confused by a variety of different names being used by the same offices throughout the relatively short period of the occupation. For example, the head of the naval dockyard in Brest was called 'Arsenal Commander' until November 1940 when the title was changed to *Oberwerftdirektor* (Senior Shipyard Director) and in August 1943 it was once again changed to 'Arsenal Commander'. Adding to the confusion, the Kriegsmarine transferred a number of its traditional titles to cover the functions of similar offices abroad, which can give a misleading picture, especially to foreigners who translate the names.

Both Norway and France came under the jurisdiction of three different autonomous offices, each with their own chain of command:

1. The commanding admiral for Norway and France.
2. The U-boat arm's own administrative structure.
3. Regional commanders responsible for the defence of their area.

The reason for listing these in order here is to separate the two different main naval branches from one another by inserting the U-boats' own system between them.

NORWAY

Commanding Admiral Norway (later Marineoberkommando Norwegen*)*

The office of Commanding Admiral Norway was created in April 1940 to be responsible for naval activities in Norway including its coastal areas. On 1 February 1943 this was renamed *Marineoberkommando Norwegen* and the Commanding Admiral was promoted to Supreme Commander-in-Chief. At the same time regional admirals were promoted to cover the following areas: Polar Coast, North Coast and West Coast.

The Commanding Admiral for Norway was General Admiral Hermann Boehm (April 1940–January 1943) who remained as Supreme Commander-in-Chief until March 1943 when he was replaced by Admiral Otto Ciliax, who remained in office until one month before the end of the war when he was succeeded by Admiral Theodor Krancke.

(Hermann Boehm was the Commander-in-Chief of the High Seas Fleet from November 1938–October 1939. Otto Ciliax commanded the battleship Scharnhorst *for the first ten month of 1939, then became Commander-in-Chief of the Naval Group Command: West and then Commander-in-Chief for Battleships. Theodor Krancke commanded the pocket battleship* Admiral Scheer *from October 1939 to June 1941, for a long voyage as far as the Indian Ocean. He was the Permanent Naval Representative at Hitler's headquarters from January 1942 until March 1943 and the go-between for Grand Admiral Erich Raeder and the Führer during the crisis around Raeder's resignation following Hitler's decision to abandon the capital warships programme.)*

The staff was quite a considerable one, covering the major departments represented in the major bases.

TRONDHEIM

Commander for Sea Defences Trondheim

Initially during the invasion of Norway, a port commander was appointed to take charge of Trondheim and this post was upgraded in May 1940 as Commander for the Sea Defences of Trondheim. The area of jurisdiction included a considerable part of the coastline towards the south, stretching as far as the Finnish border in the north and including the numerous fjords as well as outlying islands.

Commanders for Trondheim:

KS	Hans Hain	April 40–May 40	(Survey ship *Meteor*)
KS	August Thiele	May 40–June 41	(Heavy cruiser *Lützow*, ex. *Deutschland*, Fleet Command: of Staff)
VA	Leopold Siemens	June 41–April 42	(Naval Attaché in London at outbreak of war)
KA	Walter Krastel	April 42–June 42	
VA	Leopold Siemens	June 42–November 44	(Naval Attaché in London at outbreak of war)
VA	Erich Schulte Mönting	November 44–end	(Supreme Commander in Chief of the Navy's Chief of Staff)

Naval Dockyard Trondheim

A naval dockyard was established shortly after the invasion of Norway and continued to function entirely under naval leadership until 1943 when much of the technical work was taken over by staff from Germania Works in Kiel. Technically the shipyard came under the jurisdiction of the Senior Shipyard Staff in Norway while the people were administered by the Admiral of the Norwegian North Coast.

Dockyard Directors:

VA	Eduard Eichel	August 40–April 43	
KS	Waldemar von Fischer	April 43–February 44	
KA(Ing)	Wilhelm Johannsen	February 44–November 44	
KS(Ing)	Heinrich Vöge	December 44–February 45	
KS(Ing)	Ludwig Moritz	February 45–end	(Served on *Hipper* and *Tirpitz* as engineering officer)

The following departments were established in the dockyard:
Equipment provision and navigation
Artillery
Ship Construction
Mechanical engineering
Harbour construction
Torpedoes
Supplies
Administration and equipment
Communications
Medical

There was also a Naval Construction Battalion in Trondheim. This was founded in Swinemünde on the German Baltic coast shortly after the beginning of the war and originally comprised entirely of men from the National Labour Service. The commanding officer, a Major Kajetan Thomas, was later promoted and given the title of Naval Pioneer Officer. Both he and his men came under the direct jurisdiction of the Admiral for the Norwegian North Coast.

U-boats

13th U-boat Flotilla
Flotilla Commander: FK   Rolf Rüggeberg   June 43–end   (U513)

Defences

Commander for the Sea Defences of Trondheim:
KS   Hans Rose   June 40–July 43
KS   Fritz Berger   July 43–end   (Z8, Commander of 1st and 5th
                                        Destroyer Flotilla)

Port Protection Flotilla Trondheim
Naval Artillery Department 506 (Trondheim–Brettingen)
        Originally founded as Naval Artillery Department Trondheim, then renamed
        Naval Artillery Department 306 in June 40 and renamed Naval Artillery
        Department 506 in July 40.
Naval Artillery Department 507 (Husöen) Founded in August 40.
32. Naval Anti-Aircraft Regiment
        Founded in October 1944 with the following units:
                Naval Anti-Aircraft Department 701
                Naval Anti-Aircraft Department 702
                Naval Anti-Aircraft Department 715
1. Naval Fog Making Department.

BERGEN

Bergen came under the jurisdiction of the Admiral for the Norwegian West Coast, Admiral Otto von Schrader.

Naval Dockyard Bergen

Senior Dockyard Director:

KA	Friedrich Braune	May 41–May 42
KA	Waldemar Bender	May 42–March 43
KA(Ing)	Alfred Schulze	March 43–end

The following main departments were represented:

Central Department
Equipment provision and supplies
Artillery
Technical office
Harbour construction
Administration
Medical

U-boats

11th U-boat Flotilla
Flotilla Commander:

FK	Hans Cohausz	May 42–December 44	(UA, U30)
FK	Heinrich Lehmann-Willenbrock	December 44–end	(U8, U5, U96, U256)

Commander for the Sea Defences of Bergen

The area of the Commander for Sea Defences Bergen stretched for a considerable distance north and south and included the numerous fjords along the coast, as well as the outlying islands. Unlike France, where co-operation with the locals was considerably better, it was necessary to maintain considerably tighter security of both the coast and the individual defence installations These problems were brought to a dramatic climax in April 1944, at about the same time as the famous assassination attempt on Hitler, when an act of sabotage in the form of a massive explosion killed several of the staff and wounded the port commander, Walther Oehler, so seriously that he was discharged from the navy on 31 January 1945.

Commander for Sea Defences Bergen:

KS	Heinrich Ruhfus	April 40–August 40	(Light cruiser *Königsberg*)
KS	Walther Strasser	August 40–May 42	
KS	Wilibald Schmidt	May 42–September 42	
FK	Dr. Moraht	September 42–December 43	
KA	Walther Oehler	December 43–August 44	
KS	Ludolf von Hohnhorst	April 44–August 44	
KS	Georg Wildemann	August 44–September 44	
KA	Clamor von Trotha	September 44–January 45	
KS	Oskar Schomburg	January 45–end	(U26, F.d.U. East)

Port Protection Flotilla Bergen
Naval Artillery Department 504 at Gravdal.
> Founded in April 1940 as Naval Artillery Department Bergen, re-named in June 1940 as Naval Artillery Department 304 and a month later as Naval Artillery Department 504.

31st Naval Anti-Aircraft Regiment (Bergen).
> Founded in October 44 with:
> > Naval Anti-Aircraft Departments 802 founded in June 1940,
> > Naval Anti-Aircraft Department 822, founded in November 44

31st Naval Fog Making Department.

FRANCE

BREST

Naval Arsenal/Dockyard

Commanding Officer:

KK	August Vollheim	June 40–November 40
VA	Hans-Herbert Stobwasser	December 40–May 43
VA	Alfred Schirmer	May 43–September 43

The following Departments were represented:
Equipment provision
Supplies
Artillery
Ship building
Mechanical engineering
Technical staff

Harbour construction
Torpedo
Communications
Administration
Personnel
Medical

U-boats

1st U-boat Flotilla: Founded originally in Kiel and later moved to Brest. Disbanded during September 44.
Flotilla Commander:

KK	Hans Eckermann	January 40–October 40	(UA, U20)
KK	Hans Cohausz	October 40–February 42	(U30, UA)
KL	Heinz Buchholz	February 42–July 42	(U24, U15, U195, U177)
KK	Werner Winter	July 42–September 44	(U22, U103)

9th U-boat Flotilla: Founded in November 41 and disbanded in August 44.
Flotilla Commander:

| KL | Jürgen Oesten | November 41–March 42 | (U61, U106, U861) |
| KK | Heinrich Lehmann-Willenbrock | April 42–August 44 | (U8, U5, U96, U256) |

Commander for the Sea Defences of Brest

Commanding Officer:	KS	Gustav Kieseritzki	July 40–December 40
Port Commander:	FK	Erwin Kaehlert	June 40–September 44
	FK	Rudolf Westphal	February 43–April 43

Coastal Protection Flotilla Brest was founded in June 40 and renamed Port Protection Flotilla Brest in December 40.

Naval Artillery Department 262. Founded as Naval Artillery Department 203 in Ijmuiden (Holland) and moved from there to St. Malo in France before going on to Brest where it was renamed.
Naval Artillery Department 264. Founded in June 40 in Brest but moved to Lorient in July 40.

Naval Anti-Aircraft Department 231: Moved from Rendsburg (North Germany) in July 44.
Naval Anti-Aircraft Department 303. Founded in Wilhelmshaven in June 40 and then moved to Brest via Breda (Holland).
Naval Anti-Aircraft Department 304. Founded in Breda (Holland) during July 40 and moved to Brest in November 40.

Naval Anti-Aircraft Department 805: Moved from Holland.
Naval Anti-Aircraft Department 811: Founded in Emden (North Germany) in January 42.

3rd Naval Fog Making Department: Founded in August 1941 in Brest and moved to Kiel during early 1943.
4th Naval Fog Making Department: Founded early in 1943.
14th Naval Motorised Transport Department: Founded September 41.
3rd Radio Location Department: Founded September 42.

LORIENT

Naval Arsenal/Dockyard

Commanding Officer:

KK(Ing)	Waldemar Seidel	July 40–August 40
VA	Hans-Herbert Stobwasser	August 40–October 40
VA	Walter Matthiae	October 40–end

Departments:
Equipment provision and supplies
Artillery
Ship building
Mechanical engineering
Harbour construction
Torpedo
Administration
Personnel
Medical
Planning office for large Atlantic shipyards
(The Commanding Admiral for France appointed an adviser for the building of large naval installations, but it quickly became apparent that there would be no great surface ship activity and therefore the original plans were changed to concentrate on the services required by U-boats.)

U-boats

2nd U-boat Flotilla: Originally in Wilhelmshaven and then both there and in Lorient, but from June 41 only in Lorient.
Flotilla Commander:

KK	Werner Hartmann	January 40–May 40	(U26, U198)
KK	Heinz Fischer	January 40–September 41	(U29)

| KK | Viktor Schütze | October 41–January 43 | (U19, U11, U25, U103) |
| KS | Ernst Kals | January 43–end | (U130) |

Werner Hartmann was also commanding U37 while leading this flotilla and Heinz Fischer stood in for him on land while Hartmann was at sea.

10th U-boat Flotilla: Founded during January 42 and disbanded in October 44.
Flotilla Commander:

| KK | Günter Kuhnke | January 42–October 44 | (U125) |

Port Defences

Port Commander:

KK	Friedrich Bacermann	June 40–January 41
KS	Franz Guilleaume	January 41–September 41
KS	Rudolf Zentner	September 41–February 44
FK	Helmut Klügel	February 44–end

Coastal Protection Flotilla: Later renamed Port Protection Flotilla
20th Naval Anti-Aircraft Regiment: Founded in August 41 from a number of existing units and renamed IV. Naval Anti-Aircraft Brigade in April 43.
Naval Anti-Aircraft Department 704
Naval Anti-Aircraft Department 708: Established in Kiel in April 42 and shortly afterwards moved to France.
Naval Anti-Aircraft Department 806
Naval Anti-Aircraft Department 807: Founded in Cuxhaven – Altenwalde during February 41 and then moved to France.
Naval Anti-Aircraft Department 817: Founded April 43
Naval Anti-Aircraft Department 818: Founded in Lorient in March 43 and moved to Gotenhafen (East Prussia) in November 43.
Naval Artillery Department 264
Naval Artillery Department 631
Naval Artillery Department 633
Naval Artillery Department 638
3rd Naval Fog making Department: Founded during February 43 in Kiel – Surendorf and moved to Lorient in May 43. Moved once again in October 43 to Swinemünde (Germany).
8th Minesweeping Flotilla
14th Submarine Chaser Flotilla
Port Protection Flotilla

ST NAZAIRE

Naval Dock Yard

Commanding Officer:

VA	Wolf von Trotha	(January 41–October 42)
VA	Witold Rother	(October 42–end)
VA(Ing)	Ernst Stieringer	(Dockyard closed before he took up office)

Departments:
- Equipment provision
- Artillery
- Ship building
- Mechanical engineering
- Harbour construction
- Torpedo
- Communications
- Supply
- Administration
- Personnel
- Medical

U-boats

6th U-boat Flotilla: Moved to St. Nazaire from Danzig in February 42.
Flotilla Commander:

KL	Fritz Frauenheim	Appointment not taken up	(U21, U101)
KK	Georg-Wilhelm Schulz	September 41–October 43	(U64, U124)
KL	Carl Emmermann	October 43–August 44	(U172, U3037)

7th U-boat Flotilla: Until October 40 both in Kiel and St. Nazaire, but from June 41 only in St. Nazaire.
Flotilla Commander:

KK	Hans Rösing	January 40–May 40	(U11, U35, U48, FdU: West)
KK	Herbert Sohler	May 40–February 44	(U10)
KK	Adolf Piening	March 44–end	(M72, M2, U155)

Port Defences

Port Commander: KS   Ernst Kellermann   June 40–end
Port Protection Flotilla
Naval Artillery Department 280
Naval Artillery Department 282
Naval Artillery Department 684

22nd Naval Anti-Aircraft Regiment: Founded in November 41 from a variety of units in the area and renamed V. Naval Anti-Aircraft Brigade in April 43.

Naval Anti-Aircraft Department 703: Founded in Vlissingen (Holland) in June 40 and moved to France in October 41.

Naval Anti-Aircraft Department 705: Founded in May 41 from Naval Anti-Aircraft Department – Koch.

Naval Anti-Aircraft Department 809: Founded in Nantes and then moved to St Nazaire in October 43.

Naval Anti-Aircraft Department 819: Founded in St. Nazaire in March 43 and moved to Toulon in December 43.

Naval Anti-Aircraft Department 820: Founded in May 43.

6th Naval Fog Department: Founded in August 43.

24th Naval Motorised Transport Department

1st Naval Communications Department

LA PALLICE

Naval Dockyard

Commanding officer:

VA	Franz Wieting	July 41–September 41
KS	Waldemar von Fischer	August 41–December 41
KA	Herbert Goehle	December 41–November 43
KA(Ing)	Waldemar Kober	November 43–December 44
KS(Ing)	Walter Türke	December 44–end

Departments:
Equipment provision and Supplies
Artillery
Ship building
Mechanical engineering
Harbour construction
Torpedo
Administration
Personnel
Medical

U-boats

3rd U-boat Flotilla
Flotilla Commander:

KK	Hans Rösing	March 41–June 41	(U11, U35, U48, FdU: West)

KL	Herbert Schultze	June 41–March 42	(U48)
KL	Heinz von Reiche	March 42–June 42	(U17)
KK	Richard Zapp	June 42–October 44	(U66)

Port Defences
Port Commander for La Pallice and La Rochelle:

KK	Rudolf Nordmann	August 40–May 41
KS	Ernst Killmann	May 41–October 43
KK	Walther Bender	February 43
FK	Helmut Westphal	April 43–June 43
FK	Arnold Rümann	June 43–September 43
KK	Erwin de Terra	September 43–end

Naval Artillery Department 684
Naval Artillery Department 687
Naval Anti-Aircraft Department 812
Naval Motorised Transport Department
Naval Regiment John
Naval Regiment Zapp

BORDEAUX

Naval Dockyard/Arsenal

Commanding officer:

KA	Siegfried Punt	July 42–November 42
KA	Heinrich Wagner	November 42–January 44
KA(Ing)	Carl Weber	January 44–August 44

Departments:
  Equipment provision and Supplies
  Artillery
  Ship building and mechanical engineering
  Harbour construction
  Administration
  Personnel
  Medical

U-boats

12th U-boat Flotilla: Founded during October 42 and disbanded in August 44.
Flotilla Commander: KK   Klaus Scholtz   October 42–August 44   (U108)

Port Defences

Port Commander: KK   Alois Stock   July 40–February 41
                     KK   Albert Benecke   February 41–August 41
                     KK   Ernst Kühnemann   August 41–August 44

Port Protection Flotilla
2nd Sperrbrecher Flotilla later used to create the Naval Battalion Tirpitz
Naval Artillery Department 284
Naval Artillery Department 618
16th Naval Motorised Transport Department
Naval Battalion Narvik made up from remnants of the 8th Destroyer Flotilla.

APPENDIX 2
Important Signals

THE FIFTH U-BOAT FLOTILLA IN KIEL

Anybody thinking that it was just a matter of U-boats turning up at a base and instantly being provided with facilities must remember that Germans are sticklers for regulations. Some of these were so comprehensive that the 5th U-boat Flotilla in Kiel produced a booklet containing the essential information for everybody calling at the base. It might be interesting to reproduce it here more or less in its entirety. A good number of the categories were repeated in the various sections and some of these repetitions have been omitted.

The flotilla was unique inasmuch that it was set up for the purpose of supplying new operational boats with the basic necessities for their first war patrol. Therefore, the majority of wartime commissioned boats passed through it.

IMPORTANT SIGNALS FOR U-BOATS CALLING ON THE 5TH U-FLOTILLA (U-BOAT BASE KIEL)

Flotilla Commander:

Kptlt. Karl-Heinz Moehle   Telephone: 97/24590   Home: 9769
As from 15 August 1941 the 5th U-Flotilla (Fitting out Flotilla) has taken over the administration of the U-boat base in Kiel. The offices can be found aboard the accommodation ship *St. Louis* which can be reached by telephone day and night on 97/24251.

THE 5TH U-FLOTILLA'S RESPONSIBILITIES

1. Fitting out new boats for their first operational cruise.
2. Looking after all submarines lying in Kiel.
3. Home flotilla for U11, UD1, UD2, UD3, UD4 and UD5.

SHIPS AND BUILDINGS BELONGING TO THE 5TH FLOTILLA

1. Accommodation ship *St Louis* with the offices for the staff of the 5th U-Flotilla, U-boat quarters 25–34, radio room and telex connections.
2. Accommodation ship *Sierra Cordoba* with U-boat quarters 35–44.
3. Accommodation ship *Ubena* with U-boat quarters 45–45.
4. Accommodation ship, the cruiser *Hamburg* with naval prison and storage facilities for goods to and from U-boats.
5. Barracks 1–4 with U-boat quarters 1–24.
6. Staff building with officers mess for officers accommodated in the barracks.

ARRIVALS AND DEPARTURES

Boats which are intending to run into Kiel and wishing to make use of the facilities should inform the 5th U-Flotilla before leaving their previous port of call. On arrival in Kiel they should report to the signal station *St Louis* (Morse recognition letters LC) and departing boats should make a similar announcement. If the boat has been booked in by telex then the signal station will immediately provide accommodation details by Morse lamp.

Having made fast in the Tirpitz Harbour, the U-boat commander should report immediately to the Commander of the 5th U-Flotilla aboard the *St Louis* and the engineering officer should report to the Flotilla's Engineer. If the boat is going to remain in dock for any length of time then the LI (Engineering Officer) should report to the Flotilla Engineer at least once every two days. Watch officers should consult the Flotilla's Adjutant (Lt.z.S. Burkhard Heusinger von Waldegg) to assure that the necessary stores are provided before the boats leaves.

All boats which leave the Inner Förde must report to the Adjutant during normal office hours or to the Duty Officer at all other times to obtain details of the latest information about mines and to be advised about the best route to take.

All boats must man the radio room at least half an hour before departure and switch on to the U-boat safety wavelength.

All boats in the Baltic must anchor at once if a prohibition is issued for their intended route and they must wait where they are until they receive further instructions.

BERTH ALLOCATION

1. A large number of berths in the Tirpitz Basin with the exception of York and Lützow Piers belong to the U-boat Arm. Berths are not allocated on a permanent basis.
2. The berths by the torpedo loading bays and to the west of the U-boat Pier may only be occupied by prior application because these are reserved especially for boats being loaded for their first war patrol.

3. The signal station *St Louis* has instructions to ask for the numbers of inward and outward going boats so that their location can be made available to inquirers. (The boat numbers were secret and the usual identification was by commander's name. This led to some confusion at times for U139 and U93, which were commanded by Horst Elfe and the last dot of Morse code, representing the final letter 'e', was sometimes missed so people thought they were dealing with U-Elf (11).)
4. Berths can be reserved for unloading and loading by prior application.
5. All commanders are reminded that there is an order from the Commander-in-Chief for U-boats that submarines may not make fast by the side of another boat. (This was to make them smaller targets for attacking aircraft.)

SAFETY

All boats in the Baltic must remain tuned to the U-boat safety wavelength and the rules for transmitting surfacing and diving reports must be strictly followed.

REQUESTS FOR ESCORTS

U-boats travelling from Kiel to North Sea ports must apply for escort at least two days before departure. Failure to do this could lead to long delays for which commanders will be held responsible.

ACCOMMODATION

Sorting out accommodation is the responsibility of Kptlt Rudolf von Singule (Telephone 97/24501). U-boat commanders are responsible that the crew is acquainted with the rules for living in official accommodation and that these rules are strictly adhered to.

RULES FOR THE ACCOMMODATION SHIPS *ST LOUIS*, *SIERRA CORDOBA* AND *UBENA*

I. Accommodation

1. Allocation of rooms will be carried out by staff aboard the ships. It is prohibited to occupy rooms which have not been allocated by them.
2. The commander will be handed details of the room allocation upon arrival in Kiel.
3. Linen, room accessories and keys are to be obtained from the resident staff and must be handed back before departure.
4. Officer and non-commissioned officer rooms will be cleaned by civilian staff. Therefore it is necessary for keys to be left with the resident staff when leaving the accommodation.

5. Petty officers and men must clean their own rooms and leave them in a tidy state when leaving.
6. Civilian clothing is prohibited in the messes.
7. Boats leaving for periods of more than six days must notify the resident staff 24 hours before departure.

II. General Rules

1. Naval personnel may not enter the rooms and passages allocated to civilian staff.
2. Smoking in the corridors is strictly forbidden.
3. Loitering near and inside cupboards is prohibited.
4. Drinks must be consumed in the 'public rooms' and may not be taken into the bedrooms.
5. The officer and warrant officer messes are open until midnight, the common room until 2300 hours. The common room for other ranks closes at 2200 hours.
6. Silence is to be observed from 2200 hours.

III. Catering

U-boat crews will be provided with the food of the day if they have applied for it and this must be collected from the kitchens. Meal times are as follows:
Breakfast 0700–0800, Lunch 1130–1230, Evening meal 1700–1800.
Should official duty prevent these times being adhered to then the resident staff must be informed before hand.

IV. Blackout

1. Once an air raid warning has sounded all occupants of the accommodation ships are woken and will remain fully clothed in their rooms.
2. The alarm bells will sound if the ship is in danger of attack and it must then be vacated as quickly as possible. Everybody will immediately make their way to shelters on land.

V. Visitors

1. Naval personnel are only allowed to receive civilian visitors if permission has been granted and if the visitors have the appropriate passes.
2. Civilian visitors must leave the ships by 1900 hours, although exceptions can be made if special permission has been previously obtained.
3. Female visitors may not be taken into the bedrooms.

RULES FOR BARRACKS 1–4

I. Accommodation

1. Both U-boat and flotilla staff are accommodated in the barracks.
2. Bedrooms and storerooms will be allocated together with air raid shelter space.
3. No one is allowed to occupy rooms which have not been allocated to them by the resident staff.
4. Linen and cleaning apparatus will be handed out to each dormitory and must be handed back in good order. The eldest man in each room is responsible to see that this is done.
5. U-boat crews are responsible for the daily cleaning of their rooms.
6. All personal property is to be locked in cupboards. Anything found lying around will be confiscated and the owners will be punished because they are encouraging others to steal. Each cupboard is to be marked with name, rank and boat's number.

II. Guard Duties

The entire barrack area is guarded by resident staff which also employs people for telephone duty.

III. General Rules

1. There will be silence in the barracks from 2200 hours.
2. Taking drinks into the bedrooms is forbidden.
3. Washrooms, lavatories and bathrooms are to be left in a proper and orderly state.

IV. Blackout

1. The room eldest is responsible that each room is blacked out.
2. Blackout in corridors, washrooms, lavatories, common rooms etc. is dealt with by the resident staff.

V. Air Raid Alarm

Fire watchers will take up their positions quickly and all other soldiers are to take the shortest route to their allocated positions in the air raid shelters.

OFFICER ACCOMMODATION RULES

I. Accommodation

1. The main staff building also serves as accommodation base for commanders and officers from the base and from U-boats.

2. Clearing up rooms and cleaning them is dealt with by members of the crew and the cleaning of all other areas is done by the resident staff.

II. General Rules

1. There will be silence in the accommodation blocks from 2300 hours onwards.
2. Drinks may not be taken into the bedrooms.

III. Visitors

Visitors are allowed during the week from 1700–1900 hours and Sundays 1400–1900 hours. Visitors outside these hours need a pass from the duty officer. A special Ladies Room has been provided for female visitors so that their presence does not interfere with colleagues who wish to remain undisturbed.

IV. Mess Arrangements

1. The officers' mess is open to all officers and officials of the base and officers from U-boats.
2. Meal times are as follows: Breakfast 0700–0900, Lunch 1200–1400, Evening meal 1800–2000.
3. Magazines and newspapers in the common rooms are there for everybody and may not be removed, even with the intention of returning them very quickly.
4. To comply with national law, alcoholic drinks may not be served after 2300 hours.
5. It is prohibited to bring dogs into the officers' mess.
6. When air raid warnings sound everybody must make their way into shelters as quickly as possible. The most senior officer is responsible for assuring that no one remains in the mess.

TECHNICAL MATTERS

All technical matters and queries are to be discussed with flotilla's engineer and it is necessary to arrange times for the delivery of torpedoes, ammunitions, provisions, compensating compasses, degaussing etc. and at least 2–3 days notice is required. All trials must be booked in advance before every operational voyage and after any spell in the dockyard.

TRANSPORT MATTERS

1. The transport of goods for all outward bound boats is controlled by Stabsbootsmann Krause aboard *St Louis*, telephone 24251, extension 9.

2. At least two days before departure, all boats should provide a list of goods to be transported. This should include the total number of boxes or other packages which have to be moved and where they should be sent to. The outside of such packages must be marked with name, naval number, boat's number. It is necessary that all such goods are handed over personally to the transport department of the 5th U-Flotilla. Clear labels are essential, especially as the goods have to be transferred several times without any of the workers being aware of their destination.

ADMINISTRATION ASSISTANCE

1. Pay with diving supplement Boats from other ports should hand in a crew list to the flotilla's pay office. Commanders are responsible that signed receipts are handed back to the flotilla's office as quickly as possible after the men have been paid.
2. The supply of equipment and consumables: All requests for portable equipment and consumables must be recorded in the appropriate book and signed by the commander and by the responsible officer from the 5th U-Flotilla.

Repairs and/or other work on and in the boat will only be carried out if the request has been signed by the commander and approved by the flotilla engineer.

DISCIPLINE

1. While in Kiel the commanding officer of the 5th U-Flotilla will be the immediate senior officer and this also applies to boats from other flotillas which happen to call.
2. Officers must apply for leave at the Flotilla Commander's office and also report there before leaving and immediately upon returning.

GUARD DUTIES AND AIR RAID ORDERS

(These apply also to dockyard workers)
1. Special watch officers are responsible for guarding boats in the Tirpitz Basin and in the adjoining ship yards. Men eligible for such duties are: watch and engineering officers up to the rank of Oberleutnant. The duty guard officer must collect the Report Book from the office aboard *St Louis* before 2000 hours. The times for patrols are given in the book. The Report Book should be handed in at the office before 0900 hours.
2. Each watch must consist of at least 2 warrant officers and three men. Aboard smaller boats this can be reduced to one warrant officer and three men.
3. There must be an armed guard with pistol guarding each boat after hours.
4. All hatches, except the main conning tower hatch are to be kept closed at night.

5. No lights are to be shown on or from the conning tower. Screened lights for illuminating walkways are permitted but these must be switched off as soon as the air raid sirens are sounded.

6. During an air raid everybody inside the submarine is to be woken up and be ready to combat incendiaries which might fall near the boat. All internal bulkheads are to be closed and the men must assemble in the central control room. One man will keep watch from the conning tower.

MEDICAL ATTENTION

Arrangements should be made for the entire crew to be medically examined at least seven days before departure.

POST

All official and personal outgoing post should be handed in to the office aboard *St Louis*. At the same time post for the boat can be collected. Before leaving Kiel it is necessary to inform the post room aboard *St Louis* of the boat's field post number and the destination where future mail is to be sent, otherwise mail will remain in Kiel.

CINEMA TIMES

St Louis for officers: Tuesdays, Thursdays and Sundays at 2000 hours.
St Louis for other ranks: Wednesdays, Fridays and Sundays at 1830 hours.
Sierra Cordoba for officers: Mondays, Wednesdays and Fridays at 2000 hours.
Sierra Cordoba for other ranks: Mondays, Tuesdays and Thursdays at 1830 hours.
    For other entertainment see the blackboard.

LEAVE IN KIEL

Leave is allocated according to rules from the Supreme Command of the Armed Forces Number 4477 AWA?W Allg. (IIa) of 29 July 1941 and rules from Supreme Command of the Armed Forces AMA M Defence II f B Number 9042 of 6 August 1941.

DEPARTMENTS AND SECTIONS WITHIN THE 5TH U-FLOTILLA

Flotilla Commander: Kptlt Karl-Heinz Moehle
                               Tactics, communications with commanders, most senior
                               officer for all disciplinary matters.

Staff Officer:	Korvkpt Lamprecht General discipline, legal matters, defence, loss and damage to boats and equipment, crew matters, boat routines.
Adjutant:	Lt.z.S. Burkhard Heusinger von Waldegg Divisional commander, secret and other flotilla registrations, current correspondence, war diaries, sailing officer.
Secretarial officer:	Oblt.z.S. (Naval Artillery) George Correspondence, matters relating to officers, awards and medals, traditions, press and public relations.
Armaments and Equipment Officer:	Oblt.z.S. Witte Fitting out for front boats and other equipment matters.
Flotilla Engineer:	Kptlt(Ing.) Schulze Technical matters and technical staff.
2nd Engineer:	Oblt.z.S.(Ing.) Henningsmeier U-boats and oil inspections.
3rd Engineer:	Lt.z.S.(Ing.) Weiskopf Mechanical secretary, auxiliary ships and boats and their crews.
Flotilla Administrations Officer:	Kptlt(Admin) Klein Officer in charge of domestic arrangements, provisions and supplies, welfare.
2nd Administrations Officer:	Lt.z.S.(Admin) Biereichel Treasurer, officers' pay, travel expenses, removal costs.
3rd Administrations Officer:	Oberfähnrich zur See (Admin) Krüger Clothing and uniforms, emergency assistance, support.
Flotilla Medical Officer:	Stabsarzt Dr von Gregory Health matters.
2nd Medical Officer:	Dr Omerzu Medical equipment and facilities aboard U-boats, gas protection.
Communications Officer:	Oberfunkmeister Riemann Communication matters, training U-boat personnel, sound detection matters, telex.
Torpedo Officer:	Obermaschinist (Torpedo) Wiest Torpedo and mine matters.
Accommodation Ship Officer *St Louis*:	Stabsbootsmann Krause Transport of personal items belonging to U-boat men.
Accommodation Ship Officer *Sierra Cordoba*:	Kptlt Rudolf von Singule Accommodation allocation, discipline in flotilla accommodation, air raid protection, officer responsible for the barracks.

Accommodation Ship Officer
Ubena and *Hamburg*:

Lt.z.S. Schmidt
Divisional officer aboard *Ubena* and accommodation for resident flotilla staff.

Chief Flotilla Navigator:

Stabsobersteuermann Fleige
Navigation, information about mines and minefields and routes.

Commander of *Memel*:

Stabsobersteuermann Eschger
Sport.

Flotilla's Carpenter:

Oberzimmermeister Datow
Divers and diving.

Flotilla's Chief Mechanic:

Mechaniker(Artilery) Küchler
Artillery matters.

Flotilla's Chief Artificer:

Oberfeuerwerker Winkel
Munitions matters.

Non-Secret Registrar:

Oberfeldwebel Küsters
All non-secret registrations, weddings etc.

Secret Registrar:

Feldwebel Jahn
Secret communications, provision and equipment documents, details of missions etc.

APPENDIX 3

The Basic Dimensions

Atlantic and Baltic U-boat Bases with Bunkers which could accommodate U-boats. (Midget submarine accommodation has not been included.)

Town	Bunker	Lgth	Wdth	Ps	Year	Comments
Trondheim	Dora I	153	105	5–7	1941	
	Dora II	168	102	4–6	1942	Not completed
Bergen	Bruno	131	144	6–9	1941	
Kiel	Kilian	176	79	2–12	1941	
	Konrad	163	35	*	1942	
Hamburg	Elbe II	137	62	2–6	1940	
	Fink II	151	153	5–15	1941	
Bremen – Farge	Valentin	425	100	*	1943	Not completed
Bremen – Port	Hornisse	362	69	2–8	1944	Not completed
Heligoland	Nordsee III	155	88	3–9	1940	
Brest	(No Name)	193	333	15–20	1941	
Lorient	Keroman I	404	146	5–5	1941	
	Keroman II	404	146	7–7	1941	
	Keroman III	188	152	7–13	1941	
	Dombunker (E)	81	16	1	1941	
	Dombunker (W)	81	16	1	1941	
	Scorff Bunker	130	48	2–4	1941	
St. Nazaire	(No Name)	291	125	14–20	1941	
	Bunkered Lock	155	25	1	1941	
La Pallice	(No Name)	200	196	10–13	1941	
	Bunkered Lock	167	26	1	1941	
Bordeaux	(No Name)	232	160	11–15	1941	
	Bunkered Lock	175	35	1	1941	Not completed

The dimensions have been rounded off to the nearest metre. Some of the figures have been determined by converting from British yards and feet to metres, which could explain the few minor discrepancies with previously published details

Key:
Lgth	=	Length (metres)			(Type XXVII B) and Valentin
Wdth	=	Width (metres)			was due to have accommodated a
Ps	=	Number of pens and the maximum			production line for the assembly
		number of U-boats accommodated			of Type XXI boats
Year	=	Year when building work started	E	=	East
*	=	Konrad was used to build midget	W	=	West
		submarines of Type Seehund	(No Name)	=	The bunker had no official name.

Bibliography

'U-boat Bases', *After the Battle* – Number 55, Battle of Britain Prints Ltd., London, 1987. (This excellent production about the French Atlantic U-boat bases has a unique place in history by being one of the first to provide a highly illustrated account and its 'modern' photos now show a fascinating intermediate stage between the war and present day use.)

'The Raid on Saint-Nazaire', *After the Battle* – Number 59, Battle of Britain Prints Ltd., London, 1988. (An excellent publication filled with essential information and fascinating photographs.)

Arata, Contre-Amiral. *Les Villas de Kernevel*, 1997.

Aschenbeck, Nils. *Fabrik für Ewigkeit*, Junius Verlag, 1995.

Beesley, Patrick. *Very Special Intelligence*, Hamish Hamilton, London, 1977 and Doubleday, New York, 1978. (An interesting book dealing with Admiralty Intelligence.)

Berd, Jean Le. *Lorient sous l'Occupation*, Quest, France 1986.

Bohn, Roland. *1940–1945 . . . En Bretagne Consequences Economiques et Sociales de la Presence Allemande*, Privately published in Brest.

Braeuer, Luc. *La Base Sous-Marine de Saint-Nazaire*. Published privately.

Brickhill, Paul. *The Dam Busters*, Evan Bros. Ltd., London, 1951. (Rather one-sided, with information about the bombing of U-boat pens.)

Brunswig, Hans. *Feuersturm über Hamburg*, Motorbuch Verlag, Stuttgart, 1992. (An excellent book with harrowing photographs by a wartime fire-fighter.)

Busch, Rainer and Röll, Hans-Joachim. *Der U-Boot-Krieg 1939 bis 1945*. Vol 1, *Die deutschen U-Boot-Kommandanten*, Koehler/Mittler, Hamburg, Berlin, Bonn, 1996. Published in English by Greenhill as *U-boat Commanders*. (Brief biographies produced from the records of the German Deutsches U-Boot-Museum. Sadly the English edition has been published without the numerous corrections recorded by the Museum.)

——. *Der U-Boot-Krieg 1939–1945*, E.S. Mittler & Sohn, Hamburg, Berlin and Bonn, 1999. (German U-boat losses from September 1939 to May 1945 from the records of the Deutsches U-Boot-Museum.)

Christochowitz, Rainer. *Die U-Boot-Bunkerwerft "Valentin"*, Donat Verlag, Bremen, 2000

Compton-Hall, Richard. *The Underwater War 1939–45*, Blandford, Poole, 1982. (The author was the Director of the Royal Navy's Submarine Museum and this is by far the best book describing life in submarines.)

Cooper, Alan. *Beyond the Dams to the Tirpitz*, Goodall Publications Ltd., London, 1991. (About the later operations of 617 Sqdr. RAF including the bombing of U-boat pens.)

Dönitz, Karl. *Ten Years and Twenty Days*, Weidenfeld & Nicolson, London, 1959.

Fahrmbacher, Wilhelm. *Lorient, Entstehung und Verteidigung des Marine-Stützpunktes 1940/1945*, Prinz Eugen Verlag, Weissenburg, 1956. (A detailed book written by a artillery general who participated in the defence of the naval base.)

Foedrowitz, Michael. *Bunkerwelter*, Ch Links Verlag, Berlin, 1998. (Contains some good photographs and reflects a true picture of the times.)

Gamelin, Paul. *Les Bases sous-marines de L'Atlantique et Leurs Défenses 1940–1945*, Editions des Paludiers, La Baule, 1981.

Herzog, Bodo. *60 Jahre deutsche Uboote 1906–1966*, J.F. Lehmanns, Munich, 1968. (A useful book with much tabulated information.)

——. *U-boats in Action*, Ian Allan, Shepperton and Podzun, Dorheim. (A pictorial book with captions in English.)

Hessler, Günter, Hoschatt, Alfred and others. *The U-boat War in the Atlantic*, HMSO, 1989.

Hirschfeld, Wolfgang. *Feindfahrten*, Neff, Vienna, 1982. (The secret diary of a U-boat radio operator compiled in the radio rooms of operational submarines. A most invaluable insight into the war and probably one of the most significant accounts of the war at sea.)

—— and Geoffrey Brooks. *Hirschfeld – The Story of a U-boat NCO 1940–46*, Leo Cooper, London, 1996. (A fascinating English language edition of Hirschfeld's life in U-boats.)

Högel, Georg. *Embleme Wappen Malings deutscher Uboote, 1939–1945*, Koehlers, Hamburg, Berlin, Bonn, 1997. Published in English as *U-boat Emblems of World War II 1939–1945*, Schiffer Military History, Atglen, 1999. (An excellent work dealing with U-boat emblems, very well illustrated with drawings by the author who served in U30 and U110 during the war.)

Johr, Barbara and Roder, Hartmut. *Der Bunker*, Tennen, Bremen, 1989.

Jones, R.V. *Most Secret War*, Coronet, London, 1978.

Jung, D., Maass, M. and Wenzel, B. *Tanker und Versorger der deutschen Flotte 1900–1980*, Motorbuch, Stuttgart, 1981. (This excellent book is the standard reference work on the German supply system.)

Koop, G., Galle, K. and Klein F. *Von der Kaiserlichen Werft zum Marinearsenal*, Bernard & Graefe Verlag, Munich, 1992.

Lohmann, W. and Hildebrand, H.H. *Die deutsche Kriegsmarine 1939–1945*, Podzun, Dorheim, 1956–1964. (This multi-volume work is the standard reference document on the German Navy, giving details of ships, organisation and personnel.)

McCartney, Innes. *Submarine Wrecks of the English Channel*, Underwater World Publications, London, 2001

Middlebrook, Martin and Everitt, Chris. *The Bomber Command War Diaries*, Viking, New York, 1985. (A useful reference book.)

Ministry of Information, *Combined Operations 1940–1942*, HMSO, 1943.

Müller, Reinhold. *Unter weisser Flagge – St. Nazaire 1944–45*, Podzun Verlag, Bad Nauheim, 1966.

Mulligan, Timothy P. *Neither Sharks Nor Wolves*, United States Naval Institute Press, Annapolis, 1999 and Chatham Publishing, London 1999. (An excellent book about the men who manned the U-boats.)

Naval Intelligence Division. *Germany, Volume III* and *IV*, Geographical Handbook Series, Ministry of Defence, London 1944 & 1945.

——. *France, Volume IV*, Ministry of Defence, London 1942. (These official books for restricted circulation are excellent and copies are sometimes available in second-hand bookshops.)

Neitzel, Sönke. *Die deutschen U-bootbunker und Bunkerwerften*, Bernard & Graefe Verlag, Koblenz, 1991. (A standard reference book on the subject with good photographs and useful maps and interesting diagrams.)

OKM (Supreme Naval Command). *Rangliste der deutschen Kriegsmarine*, Mittler & Sohn, published annually, Berlin.

——. *Handbuch für U-boot-Kommandanten*, Berlin, 1942. Re-printed by Thomas Publications, Gettysburg, 1989.

Pallud, Jean-Paul. *Les sous-marins allemands – 2. Les Bases*, Editions Heimdahl, 1989.

Raeder, Erich. *Struggle for the Sea*, William Kimber, London, 1959.

——. *My Life*, United States Naval Institute, 1960; translation of *Mein Leben*, F. Schlichtenmayer, Tübingen, 1956.

Rohde, Jens. *Die Spur des Löwen U1202*, Libri Books on Demand, Itzehoe, 2000. (A different type book with very little text but a great deal of interesting original documentation and photographs.)

Rössler, Eberhard. *Die deutschen U-boote und ihre Werften*, Bernard & Graefe, Koblenz, 1979.

——. *Geschichte des deutschen U-bootbaus*, Bernard & Graefe, Koblenz, 1986.

Rohwer, J. and Hümmelchen. G. *Chronology of the War at Sea 1939–1945*, Greenhill, London, 1992. (A good, solid and informative work. Well indexed and most useful for anyone studying the war at sea.)

Rolf, Rudi. *Der Atlantikwall*, AMA Verlag, Amsterdam 1983.

—— and Saal, Peter. *Fortress Europe*, Airlife, Shrewsbury 1986

Roskill, Captain S.W. *The War at Sea*, HMSO, London, 1954, reprinted 1976. (Four volumes. The official history of the war at sea, 1939–45.)

Schlemm, Jürgen. *Der U-Boot-Krieg 1939–1945*, Elbe Spree Verlag, Hamburg and Berlin, 2000 (A comprehensive and most useful bibliography of the U-boat war.)

Schmeelke, Karl-Heinz and Michael. *Deutsche-U-Bootbunker Gestern und Heute*, Waffen Arsenal, Podzun Pallas Verlag, Wölfersheim-Berstadt, 1996.

Sharpe, Peter. *U-boat Fact File*, Midland Publishing, Leicester, 1998

Showell, Jak P. Mallmann. *The German Navy in World War Two*, Arms and Armour Press, London, 1979; Naval Institute Press, Annapolis 1979 and translated as *Das Buch der deutschen Kriegsmarine*, Motorbuch Verlag, Stuttgart, 1982. (Covers history, organisation, the ships, code writers, naval charts and a section on ranks, uniforms, awards and insignias by Gordon Williamson. Named by the United States Naval Institute as 'One of the Outstanding Naval Books of the Year'.)

——. *U-boats under the Swastika*, Ian Allan, Shepperton, 1973; Arco, New York, 1973 and translated as *Uboote gegen England*, Motorbuch, Stuttgart, 1974. (A well illustrated introduction to the German U-boat Arm, which is now one of the longest selling naval books in Germany.)

——. *U-boats under the Swastika*, Ian Allan, London, 1987. (A second edition with different photos and new text of the above title.)

——. *U-boat Command and the Battle of the Atlantic*, Conway Maritime Press, London, 1989; Vanwell, New York, 1989. (A detailed history based on the U-boat Command's war diary.)

——. *Germania International*, Journal of the German Navy Study Group. Now out of print.

——. *U-boat Commanders and their Crews*, The Crowood Press, Marlborough, 1998.

——. *German Navy Handbook 1939–1945*, Sutton Publishing, Stroud, 1999

——. *U-boats in Camera 1939–1945*, Sutton Publishing, Stroud, 1999.

——. *Enigma U-boats*, Ian Allan, London, 2000.

——. *U-boats at War – Landings on Hostile Shores*, Ian Allan, London, 2000.

——. *What Britain Knew and wanted to Know about U-boats*, (Extracts from the secret Monthly Submarine Reports.) U-Boot-Archiv Yearbook, Military Publishing, Milton Keynes, 2001.

Trevor-Roper, H.R. *Hitler's War Directives 1939–1945*, Sidgwick & Jackson, London, 1964.

U-Boot-Archiv. Das Archiv, (German) The U-boat Archive (English language). (A journal published twice a year for members of FTU, U-Boot-Archiv, D-27478 Cuxhaven-Altenbruch. Please enclose two International Postal Reply Coupons if asking for details.)

Verband Deutscher Ubootsfahrer. Schaltung Küste. (Journal of the German Submariners' Association.)

Wagner, Gerhard (ed.). *Lagevorträge des Oberbefehlshabers der Kriegsmarine vor Hitler*, J.F. Lehmanns, Munich, 1972. Translated as *Fuehrer Conferences on Naval Affairs*, Greenhill, London, reprinted with new introduction 1990 (Originally the English language edition was published before the German version)

Werner, Herbert A. *Iron Coffins*, Arthur Baker Ltd., London, 1969.

Wichert, Hans Walter. *Decknamenverzeichnis deutscher unterirdischer Bauten des zweiten Weltkrieges*, Joh. Schulte, Mönchstr. 34, 34431 Marsberg, 1993.

Williamson, Gordon and Pavlovik, Darko. *U-boat Crews 1914–45*, Osprey, London, 1995. (A most interesting book with excellent colour drawings and black/white photographs.)

Wilt, Alan F. *The Atlantic Wall – Hitler's Defenses in the West 1941–1944*, The Iowa State University Press, Ames 1975.

Witthöft, Hans Jürgen. *Lexikon zur deutschen Marinegeschichte*, Koehler, Herford, 1977. (An excellent two volume encyclopaedia.)

Wynn, Kenneth. *U-boat Operations of the Second World War*, Chatham, London, 1997.

Zimmermann, R. Heinz. *Der Atlantikwall*, Schild Verlag, München 1989.

——. *Records Relating to U-boat Warfare 1939–1945*, US National Archives and Records Administration, 1985.

——. *Fuehrer Conferences on Naval Affairs 1939–1945*, Greenhill, London, 1990.

Index

Many names mentioned in various lists and obvious references in main chapters have not been indexed. Where references occur frequently throughout the same chapter, only the first entry has been indexed.

Cohausz, Hans 171, 173
Construction bunkers 21
Cooking 28
Covered locks 21
Cremer, Ali 116

Dambuster raid 138
Danzig 57
Das Boot, film 122
Deep penetration bomb 138
Deschimag AG Weser 77
Destitute children 30
Deutsche Werft 72, 134, 160
Deutsche Werke 64
Disney bombs 140
Dombunker 103, 105
Dönitz, Karl 3, 112, 122, 126, 156, 157, 162, 164
Dora I 8, 17, 22, 24, 50, 54
Dresden 131

Eade, Lt Cmdr W.N. 76
Earthquake bomb 129, 138
Eastern front 167
Eckermann, Hans 173
Edward III 86
Eichel, Eduard 169
Elbe II 3, 45, 52, 72, 150, 153, 161
Electrolysis 58
Elfe, Horst 183
Emden 151
Emmermann, Carl 176
Endrass, Engelbert 48
Enigma code 126
English Channel 167
English king 86
Entertainment programme 28

Farge 152
Farge *see* Valentin
Fink II 134, 148, 160
Fire fighters 29
Fischer Waldemar von 169, 177
Fischer, Heinz 175
Fishing Harbour 96
Fitting-out bunkers 21
Fleet Commander 42
Floating harbour 118, 125
Flyash 23
Forced labour 8
Förde 63
Frauenheim, Fritz 176
Freeport 74
French orphans 30

French submarine museum 114
Frobisher, Sir Martin 86
Fuerteventura 21

Geneva Convention 8
Germania works 151
Gironde river 122, 146
Gneisenau 88, 110
Goehle, H. 177
Göring, Hermann 3
Grand Slam 82, 134, 138, 140, 143, 152
Granite blocks 129
Grossi, Kpt. 126
Guilleaume, F. 175

Hain, Hans 169
Hamburg 23, 45, 134, 148
Hamburg, cruiser 182
Hardegen, Reinhard 67, 106
Harms, ship salvage firm 161
Hartmann, Werner 174
Hauber, Hans-Gerhold 17, 151
HDW 52, 64, 75, 151, 161
Heligoland 3, 143
Hirschfeld, Wolfgang 75
Hitler's pilot 7
HMS *Campbeltown* 110, 155, 162
HMS *Dolphin* 75
HMS *Tuna* 126
HMS *Tynedale* 160
Hohnhorst, L. von 172
Hornisse bunker 164
Horten 152
Hotel Celtic 37
Hotel Majestik 40
Hotel Royal 108
House Atlantic 33
Howaldtswerke 74

Ijmuiden 138
Ile de Groix 97
Invasion of Russia 167
Iron Coffins 143
Italian Submarine Chief 42
Italian Submarine Command 156
Italian U-boat base 126

Jean Bart 109
Johannsen, Wilhelm 169

Kaehlert, E. 173
Kals, Ernst 175
Kayak canoes 146